MICROCOMPUTERS IN THE CORPORATE ENVIRONMENT

Phillip W. Bugg

PRENTICE-HALL
Englewood Cliffs, New Jersey 07632

Library of Congress Cataloging-in-Publication Data

BUGG, PHILLIP W.
   Microcomputers in the corporate environment.

   Includes index.
   1. Business—Data processing. 2. Microcomputers.
I. Title.
HF5548.2.B7775 1986   658'.05416   85-24401
ISBN 0-13-580234-2

Editorial/production supervision and
   interior design: *Kathryn Gollin Marshak and Carol L. Atkins*
Cover design: *Whitman Studio, Inc.*
Manufacturing buyer: *Gordon Osbourne*

Printed in the United States of America

10 9 8 7 6 5 4 3 2 1

ISBN   0-13-580234-2   025

Prentice-Hall International (UK) Limited, *London*
Prentice-Hall of Australia Pty. Limited, *Sydney*
Prentice-Hall Canada Inc., *Toronto*
Prentice-Hall Hispanoamericana, S.A., *Mexico*
Prentice-Hall of India Private Limited, *New Delhi*
Prentice-Hall of Japan, Inc., *Tokyo*
Prentice-Hall of Southeast Asia Pte. Ltd., *Singapore*
Editora Prentice-Hall do Brasil, Ltda., *Rio de Janeiro*
Whitehall Books Limited, *Wellington, New Zealand*

To my mother and the memory of my father

*To Jennifer, Kimberly, and especially
Jeri, who is always there for me*

Contents

PART III   MICROCOMPUTER APPLICATIONS

PART IV MICROCOMPUTER MANAGEMENT

Preface

Although much has been written about the technical aspects of microcomputers, very little has been written about microcomputing itself. Still less has been written about how to manage the organizational aspects of microcomputing.

This lack of information on microcomputer management became obvious when my work as a consultant led me into intensive problem-solving sessions on microcomputers and their appropriate use in large organizations. In these sessions and seminars, where the topics under discussion ranged from the technical to the political, it became obvious that most of the problems encountered by companies using microcomputers were unexpected and unique. No book of guidelines for managing microcomputer resources came ready to be unpacked with the hardware and software. This was virgin territory as far as management was concerned.

But out of these sessions came a great deal of useful information. The microcomputer experiences of these companies provided valuable insight into what works and what does not work, what the useful applications of microcomputers are in a company, and what kinds of support microcomputer users require if a company is to realize the best return on its investment in the technology.

I believe that the best ideas from these sessions have found their way into this book, as the purpose of *Microcomputers in the Corporate Environment* is to serve as a guide to those using or planning to use microcomputer technology in corporate settings. It is written for all who are involved with microcomputers in business, but especially for those who are in a position of influencing, supporting, or managing corporate microcomputing resources.

Part I: An Introduction focuses briefly on the microcomputer revolution and the dynamics that account for the rapid acceptance of microcomputer technology. This section also identifies the special significance that microcomputer technology has for business and for business-information users.

Part II: Microcomputer Systems provides a brief technical description of microcomputer hardware and software. The intent of this section is to equip non-technically oriented readers with enough fundamental concepts and terminology to hold their own in a discussion with those who are more technically oriented.

Part III: Microcomputer Applications focuses on the kinds of business uses to which microcomputers can be applied on a day-to-day basis. Each of the five generic microcomputer applications—number processing, word processing, graphics, data storage and retrieval, and data communications—is discussed in depth.

Part IV: Microcomputer Management offers specific advice on microcomputer policy and on the development and management of corporate microcomputer support services. This last section also looks at whether or not a company should use microcomputer technology, and a final chapter considers microcomputer trends and what microcomputers portend for the future.

ACKNOWLEDGMENTS

It is impossible to give proper credit to everyone who has made a contribution to or assisted me in the effort of writing this book. However, I would be highly remiss if I did not acknowledge a few individuals who have made special contributions.

Dan Myers, business associate and friend, provided a seemingly endless fund in ideas, many of which found their way into the first several chapters. I am especially grateful for his enthusiasm, cheerful support, and early encouragement in the whole book-writing project.

Fred McFadden, Jim MacDonald, and Steve Karch provided useful insights and extremely helpful suggestions. To them I owe a large measure of gratitude, both for their generous spirit in sharing their expertise and for their friendly concern that they not give offense by their criticism.

Hugh Martin is a true microcomputer aficionado whose knowledge is always up to date. We have spent many enjoyable hours discussing the technology, and (perhaps unknown to him) these discussions have always been for my edification and benefit.

Don Elliott, friend and mentor, whose sense of the practical and workable never ceases to amaze me, has been especially helpful in providing critical information at just the time I needed it.

Finally, I owe a debt of gratitude to the many corporate microcomputer management "pioneers" who have learned their lessons the hard way. Their contributions in my seminars and consulting sessions have always been interesting, unfailingly relevant, and frequently more germane than my own.

Phillip W. Bugg

CHAPTER

1

The Microcomputer Revolution

We are engaged in a revolution. A microcomputer revolution. In less than a decade, the microcomputer or personal computer—call it what you will—has become a common and fashionable sight in private homes and in businesses of all types, from the corner mom-and-pop stores to the highest corporate towers. By the end of 1984, more than 8 million microcomputers had been purchased, presumably by consumers hungry for a little personal computing of their own.[1]

And a revolution it is. Up until the advent of the minicomputer and the microcomputer, virtually all computers were owned and operated by the government, universities, and larger corporations. Within these settings, the use of computers was inaccessible to all but a select few. Computing was the exclusive domain of the computing professional.

But no longer. Today, *microcomputer* is literally a household word with more than 15 percent of all American households owning one and another 20 or so percent planning to purchase one in the near future. Virtually anyone or any business can

---

[1]It is difficult to get an exact fix on just how many microcomputers actually have been bought. Eight million is the best estimate available to the author at the time of this writing, although estimates vary considerably.

now own, operate, and enjoy the advantages of these electronic data-processing marvels.

What kind of a revolution is it? A soft revolution, to be sure. Certainly not one to overthrow anything—except, perhaps, exclusivity. This revolution, the microcomputer revolution, does not seem to be a revolt so much as a rapid and dramatic surge toward more of the noncomputing community becoming an active part of the computing community.

1.1 AN UNQUALIFIED COMMERCIAL SUCCESS

The success of the microcomputer has been amazing to observers both inside and outside the data-processing and computer industry. The real astonishment is not that a microcomputer could be built technologically, but that such a computer would be a runaway commercial success.

The first commercial microcomputer was marketed in 1975 by MITS/ALTAIR as a kit for hobbyists.[2] The APPLE™ was the first ready-to-plug-in-and-compute microcomputer and its success is, of course, legendary. The APPLE was quickly followed by Tandy-Radio Shack's TRS-80™ and Commodore Business Machine's PET™, both of which were also early successes.[3]

Today there are more than 30 different brands of microcomputers on the world market, with hundreds of other manufacturers of related equipment, add-ons, and programs. The microcomputer industry has grown in less than a decade to a 27 billion dollar a year industry, and has a predicted growth rate of 20 to 25 percent compounded annually.

1.2 A NEW LITERACY

The microcomputer has placed computing within reach of a whole new segment of society. This sudden access to computing and the changes it portends have spawned an urgency for society to understand how to use computers—to be "computer literate." There is a growing belief that every educated person in the next century will need to be fully conversant and capable of using computer technology.

No one, it seems, is immune. Colleges and universities are so adamant about their students gaining computer competence that several are requiring each student to purchase his or her own personal computer. Public schools from kindergarten on up are rushing to install new courses and a computer literacy curriculum. This belief is becoming so pervasive that even parents of preschoolers are enticed by day care centers that offer "hands-on computer experiences" for *tots.*

[2]Several prototype single-use computers were built by computer manufacturers several years before the first microcomputers were offered commercially.

[3]APPLE is a registered trademark of Apple Computer, Inc. TRS-80 is a registered trademark of the Tandy Corporation. PET is a registered trademark of Commodore Business Machines, Inc.

1.3 A BUSINESS REVOLUTION TOO

The business community is experiencing its own microcomputer mania. (How could it be otherwise, with 50 percent or more of the microcomputers purchased going to major corporations.) Millions of these small computing devices are already computing away in business settings all over the world. Each business day, scores more are taken from their shipping cartons to be pressed into immediate use only hours after they have been placed in them at the factory.

Early observers and critics of the microcomputer phenomenon claimed that the microcomputer was a fad. Obviously that has not been the case. The microcomputer is now heavily employed by many sectors in addition to business including education, engineering, manufacturing, and the medical and legal professions. In fact, the microcomputer is being called the "tool of the century" because it is finding so many uses, and because it is redefining how we approach new job tasks.

Within many organizations, the flow of data and information is often a bottleneck to productivity. The microcomputer is beginning to make changes that would break these bottlenecks and move corporate operations that depend on the efficient processing of data and information to new, more productive levels.

From top-level executives on down, the microcomputer is steadily gaining a reputation as a highly useful and versatile business tool, a tool that speeds the manipulation of data, expands access to corporate information, supports in important new ways the processes of decisionmaking, and extends the brainpower and technical expertise of managers and other information workers. The microcomputer has laid a challenge at the feet of modern corporate business. That challenge is what this book is all about.

CHAPTER

2

What Drives the Revolution?

How did all this happen? Why has the microcomputer become such a phenomenon? Why the rapid acceptance? No doubt these questions will be studied and answered definitively in years to come, but even a quick study reveals that several forces conspire to make the microcomputer a legend in its own time. Four such forces can be readily identified. They are

- Advances in computer technology
- Rapidly changing business needs
- Favorable economics
- The personal nature of microcomputing itself

2.1 TECHNOLOGICAL ADVANCES

Microcomputer technology is not necessarily new technology. It is a natural, downward extension of large computer technology on a smaller scale. The development of specialized electronic circuit manufacturing techniques known as large scale integration (LSI) and very large scale integration (VLSI) makes it possible to place thousands of circuit components into a space less than one-fourth the area of a postage stamp. The circuits are photographically reduced and printed onto silicon wafers in groups. The wafers are then sliced into individual circuit *chips* and packaged in rectangular plastic housings for protection and durability. These advances have resulted in a much reduced physical size, while maintaining (or in most cases increasing) functional capability. At the same time that capability has gone up, the cost of manufacturing has gone down. It is now possible to mass produce and market these devices for only a few dollars apiece.

In the early 1970s, engineers succeeded in placing the entire logic circuitry of a computer on one of these chips. They called this special chip a *microprocessor*. The microcomputer was born when it was recognized that a single-user computer could be built using one of these microprocessors simply by adding other necessary components such as a power supply, a keyboard, a video display monitor, memory and data-storage devices, printers, and the like.

Is the technology any different than that used in large computers? Basically, no. The engineering and electronics required for the production of microcomputers are fundamentally the same as those used in large computer systems that serve multiple users. Large computers run many programs at one time and serve multiple users, and, of course, this capability adds to their size, complexity, and cost.

Unfortunately, microcomputers are sometimes perceived as toys by the public because they have been heavily advertised and popularized as devices for playing computer games. Actually, playing games accounts for only a very small percentage of the time spent using microcomputers. The prevailing image of the microcomputer as a game-playing device is out of proportion to its actual use for that purpose.

The microcomputer, like its larger relatives, is a serious, professional machine. It possesses almost phenomenal computing power for its size and cost. For single user applications, the microcomputer is functionally equivalent to a much larger *mainframe* computer.[1] This is *not* to say that a microcomputer is *equivalent* to a mainframe computer, but that for a growing number of applications, a mainframe computer can offer no significant advantages.

A point to keep in mind is that a microcomputer is not a "baby computer" waiting to grow up to become an "adult computer." Rather, it is a highly specialized "adult computer" that is totally dedicated to the computing needs of a single user with specialized computing needs.

2.2 BUSINESS NEEDS

While the development of the technology is fascinating in its own right, the development of the technology alone does not account for the microcomputer's enormous success and acceptance. Without a true need for the things that a microcom-

---

[1]The electronic components of corporate computers were originally assembled on large metal racks or frames, hence the data-processing industry's name for large computers is "mainframe."

puter can do, it would likely be nothing more than a technical curiosity. The fact of the matter is that better methods for collecting, storing, processing, retrieving, and communicating data have been needed by business professionals for some time. Long before microcomputers came on the scene, the business community was pressing for ways to meet the crushing demands of the information explosion and to improve productivity. This is particularly true in the white-collar areas of document generation, information storage and retrieval, and management decision making. Microcomputers have come along at just the right time, but if they had not, computer technology would have evolved in other directions—inevitably in ways that would serve more business information users.

To the ordinary business person, mere technical improvements in computer technology mean little. It is only as these technologies and devices are translated into business applications or into improved capabilities that the business community responds. For that reason, business uses of the microcomputer were dramatically sparked by the appearance of *generic* applications programs, such as word processing, electronic spreadsheet analysis, and business graphics.[2]

Now, more specialized business programs have been developed and made available as commercial software products. These include specialized applications in finance, accounting, budgeting, marketing, sales, inventory and warehouse management, manufacturing, cost accounting, project management, scheduling, personnel management, statistics, document generation, and others.

Perhaps the most dramatic business need for microcomputers is in the realm of management decision making. This would not seem strange but for the fact that large-scale mainframe systems have long addressed this very need. The data-processing industry has focused on providing data and information systems that would provide managers with appropriate decision information. Management information systems (MIS) were developed to provide routine and ad hoc reports to managers. The focus has been so pervasive that many data-processing departments have changed their name to MIS to reflect this fundamental corporate data-processing role. Characteristically, MIS are big systems, complex, and require substantial technical support. But while such systems have become the primary source of decision information for operations-level managers, they have not been highly successful in providing decision information to upper-level, strategic decision makers.

The reason lies in the nature of management decision making itself. Most corporate data processing involves the collection, storage, processing, and reporting of internally generated data in a more or less routine and uniform way. Operations-level managers make use of this information for monitoring corporate activities and results. Decision making at this level tends to be codified and programmatic. The decision process is straightforward and generally follows a linear path from rec-

---

[2]Generic programs are those that deal with one of our fundamental thinking symbol systems—words, numbers, and images. The generic microcomputer applications are word processing, number processing, and image processing or graphics. Also usually included in this list are data communications and data storage and retrieval.

ognition of the problem, through evaluation of the alternatives, to implementation of the solution.

Higher-level decision making, by contrast, is seldom a straightforward or linear process. Data used in strategic decisions typically are generated external to the organization and are often incomplete, and the validity and reliability of the data must constantly be questioned. The whole strategic decision process is suffused with uncertainty and involves a great deal of guesswork and business judgment.

Uncertainty in any problem situation is generally dealt with by successive approximation. A problem is identified, and tentative solutions are examined, discarded, refined, reexamined, and so on until a satisfactory solution can be found. Often the real problem itself may not be recognized until the decision process has been underway for some time. Invariably, the process of solving such problems is highly iterative, requiring many cycles of problem-solving and decision making activities.

An increasingly common approach is for decision makers to project hypothetical business situations and to ask speculative "what if . . . " types of questions, such as "What if sales double over the next six months?" or "What if the cost of raw materials increases by ten percent?" Tentative answers to these questions are obtained by using different data scenarios, by plugging those data into a model, and then by changing or "massaging" the data through several cycles until a solution "looks right" and "feels right."[3]

This iterative decision process is ideally served by the microcomputer. Changing business conditions that could potentially affect sales, costs, or any number of strategic business variables can be quickly simulated and evaluated using an electronic spread sheet or other financial modeling program. Various data sets are easily entered, calculated, changed, and recalculated, with all data relationships and interactions instantly updated. In a few hour's time, literally dozens of "what if . . . " scenarios can be modeled.

The insight provided to decision makers using this technology is enormous. The quality of decisions cannot help but be greater than it would be under other decision making circumstances simply because of the greater number of alternatives that can be considered, and the fact that simple (though potentially significant) arithmetic errors are eliminated.

The interactive nature of the microcomputer, together with appropriate modeling programs, gives users full control of all modeling activities from model selection, to data entry, to the evaluation and use of the new information. By using microcomputers, more of the whole decision information system comes under the immediate control of the decision-makers themselves.

---

[3]Strategic business decisions, even those supported by computers, are still judgment calls. It would be convenient for a computer to simply calculate a definite "right" answer, but that capability has yet to be realized and probably will not be until sometime in the distant future. Strategic decision making, even with microcomputers and other decision-support technology, still belongs to the artful, not the scientific, side of business.

2.3 FAVORABLE ECONOMICS

The economics of microcomputer ownership and operation are unquestionably an important factor in their widespread use and growth. The average purchase cost of a microcomputer system ranges between $4,000 and $8,000. This is within the scope of many private individuals and virtually all small business users.[4] It also is about on par with more traditional office equipment, and is a trivial cost when compared with similar jobs supported on large-scale computer systems. The operating costs for microcomputers in corporate settings are less clearly documented, but they seem to be modest, even for companies supporting large numbers of microcomputers.

Microcomputers and mainframes should not be compared on a cost–performance basis. They are both data processors, but they serve quite different data-processing needs. The economics of purchasing and operating large mainframe systems are different from those of purchasing and operating microcomputers because of the salary requirements for highly trained programmers and other professional staff. Payback becomes a function of operating time. To get the highest return on a large, continuing investment, mainframe computer systems are often operated around the clock.

A microcomputer, by contrast, does not incur the same kinds of operational costs, and its payback is not a function of time. A microcomputer system becomes cost-effective as soon as it returns an increase in productivity or cost savings equal to its original or amortized cost. This may happen within the first few days or weeks of operation.

A microcomputer may be used only a few hours a week and still be cost justified even though it sits unused a large share of the time. In the corporate environment where microcomputers are being used by busy, high-salaried managers, it is a far better trade-off to waste a few hours of microcomputer time than to waste even a few minutes of a manager's time. From a cost–performance perspective, it may be more meaningful to compare microcomputers to typewriters, calculators, and other traditional office technology.

Perhaps the most significant economic factor is the opportunity that microcomputers provide for increased productivity. Basically, this is accomplished by putting more personal computing capabilities directly into the hands of the information consumer.

Microcomputers increase information-worker productivity by increasing the speed, accuracy, and convenience with which data can be captured, retrieved, processed, and communicated. They allow decision makers the opportunity to examine more alternatives in less time and in greater detail than is possible without such technology.

---

[4]A microcomputer system can range from less than a $1,000 for a small portable to $10,000 or more depending on the way it is equipped. There may exist a "window" of acceptable cost. Below a certain cost, the system lacks acceptable computing capabilities. Above a certain cost, the system ceases to be a microcomputer system and becomes something more akin to a larger computer system.

The effects that microcomputers can have on productivity are difficult to estimate in hard dollars. But on a dollar-for-dollar, function-for-function basis, microcomputers in the hands of well-trained users are an unquestionable bargain. Companies that do not support their information workers with state-of-the-art information-processing tools may find themselves disadvantaged—especially when their competitors do.

2.4 MICROCOMPUTING AS A PERSONAL ACTIVITY

Finally, a very important factor contributing to the rapid acceptance of microcomputers, is the nature of microcomputing itself. When you ask users what it is they like about microcomputers you may get an equivocal answer like *"they're useful,"* *"they do the job,"* or an off-hand comment, but you are more likely to get a 25-minute dissertation on *"what a terrific machine it is"* and *"how they could never imagine doing without it."* Threatening to take away someone's microcomputer after he has become a steady user is likely to provoke a strong reaction.

The *personal attachment* that microcomputers seem to elicit from users is not altogether easy to explain. They are useful, of course, but so are the photocopier and the telephone. One seldom encounters the same kind of enthusiasm for those two devices that one typically gets from microcomputer users.

The computer—any computer—has a special, almost mystical attraction for most of us. We stand in awe (rightly so) of the microcomputer's superhuman ability to do complex calculations in microseconds or to find and retrieve a single record from among thousands on file. But the relationship between user and machine is more than simple awe.

What then is the reason for this near obsessive attachment to computers? Is it mere gadgetry? More than a few of us are easily seduced by electronic devices and gadgetry. But an infatuation with gadgets soon wears off.

Could it be because they quickly and obediently respond to our commands? It is easy to get attached to something that immediately does what we tell it to do.

Or is it simply the sense of power one gets when controlling such a complex device?

Whatever it is, the computer rewards in ways that are unrelated to the reason for computing in the first place. It is so very easy to get "caught up" in the act of computing itself.

The seductive nature of computing is no less real for microcomputer users than it is for users of large mainframe computers, but it is clear that there is something different about microcomputing, at least for the new user. Microcomputer users (even those hardened old pros who cut their teeth on megapowered mainframes) often comment that they feel less restricted and less intimidated "doing it on a micro."

Unlike a corporate mainframe system, a microcomputer does not require sign-on procedures, special access codes, and passwords. It does not keep track of how much computer time the user has used nor send the department a bill of charges at the end of the month. It does not require a cadre of highly trained professionals to program it and to keep it operating. And, because it is a stand-alone system, users feel no suspicion that "big brother" may be "watching" or keeping electronic accounts of what they are doing or how they are doing it.

If the microcomputer is a personal computer, then the mainframe must be an "impersonal computer," right? That attitude is more common than one might suspect. Mainframe computers are frequently perceived by noncomputing "outsiders" as enormously complex, inflexible, unforgiving, and difficult to learn how to use. (Not necessarily true.) These outsiders never expect to operate a large computer or, if they do, they would not expect to do so without extensive training. Many business persons have the attitude that, while computers are a useful and necessary business tool, the use of a computer terminal is the kind of activity best left to clerical staff or to the "computer people."

Microcomputing "outsiders" have a much more benign attitude toward the microcomputer. They see it as simple to operate, sufficient to their particular computing needs, and tolerant of their errors. (Also not necessarily true.) They approach microcomputers thinking they are easy to learn to use, although they may end up dedicating hours or days just getting acquainted with a single, new program. They buy into the idea that the microcomputer has been created expressly for *their kind*, that is, for the intelligent and just-slightly-ahead-of-the-times business professional.

Whether or not differences between mainframe computing and microcomputing are real or imagined, new users tend to act as though they were real, taking on faith that microcomputing is somehow qualitatively different from other forms of computing and that these differences make microcomputers appropriate for their own use.

There is yet another reason that makes microcomputers popular—one that has undoubtedly contributed to their rapid acceptance: they are *fun* to operate. Not fun, perhaps, in the same way that watching television is fun or playing pin-ball or even playing a video game is fun.[5] Like these pastimes, microcomputers provide a high degree of stimulation, but they also require a high degree of interaction and intellectual participation. Microcomputer programs (the successful ones) are easy to use but at the same time are intellectually demanding. Users seem to derive pleasure not only in coming up with solutions to their problems, but in the process of discovering or creating those solutions.

Is microcomputing fun? Ask any user.

---

[5]Interestingly, the popularity of the video game is already waning, while the popularity of microcomputers for both business and personal use continues unabated.

CHAPTER
3

Microcomputers in the Corporate Environment

Regardless of the means of its introduction into the business world or the forces that have contributed to its acceptance, the microcomputer has established a permanent place for itself on the basis of its contribution to specific business practices. To financial planners, budget strategists, market analysts, and hundreds of others, the microcomputer has become an essential tool of choice for quickly modeling and processing business information. Users of all types find that they can capture, retrieve, and process data much quicker than they could in pre-microcomputer days. The microcomputer allows decision makers to construct and examine alternatives quicker and in greater detail than ever before.

3.1 SIGNIFICANCE FOR BUSINESS

The true significance of the microcomputer is that it makes it possible for noncomputer persons to do things on a computer that once could only be done on a large computer system by highly trained computer experts. Managers can now get direct access to business data and data processing that they once could only get through computer specialists.

Direct access by managers obviates many of the problems that contribute to poor quality data and information. When information users have a hand in processing their own data, those data tend to be more relevant and do not suffer from a lack of sensitivity to the user's needs, from misinterpretation, from delays and conflicts in priorities, and from the problems that result from too much, too little, or poorly formatted information. In simple words, the microcomputer helps business users obtain better-quality information.

3.2 THE DOWN SIDE OF MICROCOMPUTERS

In the main, corporate-based microcomputers have been a success story. But despite its tremendous successes, the adoption of this technology has not been without a few thorns for corporate management. Rapid and uncontrolled proliferation has created problems and raised considerable concern for managers and users alike.

For most companies, the introduction of the microcomputer was not planned. One was purchased here, another there, several in yet another department. It was experimental, tentative technology. It came in by the backdoor and without the benefit of purchase guidelines or management controls. In rare instances, a few companies have developed their microcomputer resources with foresight and adequate planning. They have managed to avoid the problems with microcomputers that have plagued others. In the majority of cases, however, direct management of microcomputers as special corporate resources has been nil. It is usually only after a period of rapid proliferation and mounting problems that the microcomputer has commanded the serious attention of upper-level management.

The problems, along with the microcomputers, have also proliferated. A brief recital of these problems would reveal:

- Systems that do not work (and perhaps never did)
- Systems that are inadequate to the task intended
- Systems that produce low quality output
- Systems that take more effort or time than the manual systems they were designed to replace
- Systems that are not used because users were never trained to use them
- Systems that broke and could not be fixed
- Systems that distracted users from the real work to be done
- Systems that actually introduced new errors, and so on

The greatest single problem is that purchases have been made without a consideration of the work to be done or the persons who would use them. Early corporate users were not particularly concerned about how the microcomputer might someday function within a whole new corporate information system. Purchases were made without a careful analysis of the intended user's needs and the capabilities required of a new system. Seldom was a systematic comparison made of alternative computer solutions and their respective benefits. The result has been the purchase of a number of microcomputer systems that were soon outgrown, or that were marginally capable of doing the job they were intended to do in the first place.

Microcomputers have also been problematic for corporate data-processing departments. Their use by nontechnical users has often required the support and assistance of technically knowledgeable persons, and in most corporate environments those persons were data-processing professionals. In a sense, they subverted the resources of programmers, analysts, and other technical people away from the data-processing department (although, in fairness, it must be said that such assistance was usually given with the full and enthusiastic cooperation of those involved).

But there have been other problems, too. For instance, corporate microcomputer users soon discover that the data they need resides in the corporate databases. They feel justified in requesting that their microcomputer be connected to the mainframe so they can access these data, and they become annoyed when their requests to make that connection are not warmly received by data-processing managers and database administrators.

This less-than-enthusiastic response on the part of data-processing managers and database administrators is fully justified. Because in addition to some nontrivial technical problems in making the connection between microcomputer and mainframe, the problems of maintaining data confidentiality and data integrity are among the toughest problems in the computer industry. Microcomputers and microcomputer users have made those problems tougher.

The basic but understandable problem is that companies have acquired microcomputers without any prior warning of their impact, and this impact has been considerable. But it is not microcomputer technology alone that produces the problems. The whole information-processing infrastructure within organizations is changing. Microcomputers are just one component of that change, and until organizations define the appropriate roles of microcomputers within that changing information-processing infrastructure, many of the problems will continue unsolved.

This is not to imply that microcomputers are more trouble than they are worth. The evidence strongly suggests that the upside of microcomputer use has been much greater than the downside, most likely because companies have found ways to accommodate the problems introduced along with the microcomputer.

For some companies the microcomputer experience has been a disappointment, typically because of poor corporate-level planning, because expectations were set too high, or because there was inadequate support of users. For a few, the microcomputer promise has turned to microcomputer disenchantment.

3.3 MANAGEMENT INTERVENTION

It is unfortunate, but true, that some companies have felt it necessary to deal with the microcomputer problem by issuing policies specifically forbidding the use of this very useful tool. Surely less radical solutions are available.

Time will likely provide us with the perspective that these problems are not just the result of microcomputer technology, but stem from the pressures of an increasingly information-intensive world struggling to reduce the pressures by a rapid infusion of new technology. Such problems are not unexpected nor unusual in the annals of technological change, and it would be foolish to believe that microcomputers are an exception.

The solution, of course, is for management to take a more active part by intervening in ways that are appropriate. Managers might begin by focusing on these critical questions:

- Why is the company buying microcomputers?
- Who is going to use them?
- How do they fit into the existing scheme of corporate data processing and information management?
- Should the company microcompute at all?
- Should there be any controls on microcomputer use? If so, who should control them?
- How should their use be managed?
- How and by whom should microcomputer users be supported?
- What is likely to happen in the future?

These questions must inevitably be faced by each organization using micro-computer technology and, in general, the sooner the better.

4

Something
About Hardware

The management of corporate microcomputer resources requires a fairly comprehensive knowledge of the operations, capabilities, and limitations of microcomputer systems. Most managers are picked because they have this required technical knowledge. However, most corporate policymakers, the managers of the managers, are less likely to have such knowledge. While the operation of microcomputers is readily learned by those without a computer background, the terminology and jargon can be quite intimidating. This situation places the policymaker at something of a disadvantage.

It is not the purpose of this book to serve as a technical treatise on microcomputers, but this section on microcomputer systems is included to provide just enough technical information and terminology to allow the nontechnically inclined to feel less a stranger in management and policy discussions that inevitably turn technical. Readers already well versed in this area may choose to skip this chapter on hardware, and perhaps the next one on software.

4.1 WHAT A MICROCOMPUTER DOES

Computers, for all their seeming complexity, are not truly that difficult to understand. In the simplest terms, microcomputers process data. That is, they take raw data, manipulate or process them in some specific way, and give back new data in the form of documents and reports. These three activities are generally referred to as *input* (putting data into the computer), *process* (working on the data in some way so as to transform it into something more useful), and *output* (generating reports, and the like).

These three functions—Input, Process, Output—are the most fundamental activities of computing (See Figure 4.1). Everything that can be done with a computer and every piece of computer equipment can be related to one or more of these three terms. Microcomputers are no exception.

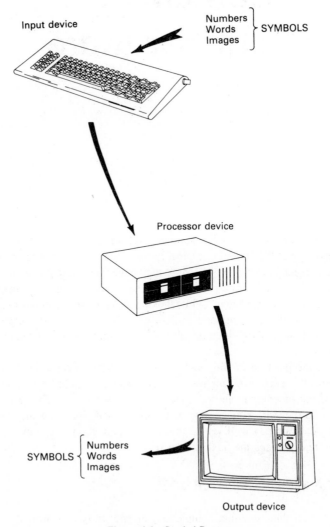

Figure 4.1   Symbol Processor

What is input, processed, and output are data in the form of numbers, words, or graphic images. So a microcomputer is three things:

- A number processor
- A word processor
- An image (graphics) processor

The microcomputer may work with these three types of information one at a time, two at a time, or all at the same time.

4.2 A NUMBERS GAME

To be technically precise, the microcomputer actually only works with numbers. When data other than a number (say letters of the alphabet or words) are entered (input) into a computer, the microcomputer immediately translates the letters into number codes, processes these numbers, and then translates the numbers back into letters. It all happens so fast that to a user it looks as though the microcomputer is working with the letters themselves.

4.3 COMPUTER PROCESSES

The microcomputer *processes* information in several different ways. It can:

- *Enter* data
- *Calculate* (add, subtract, multiply, and divide numbers)
- *Store* data for later use
- *Retrieve* data previously stored
- *Compare* data
- *Sort* lists of data in numerical or alphabetic order
- *Display* or *print* data in any format

Taken one at a time, each of these processes is quite simple. But all these processes may be combined in various ways to do complex tasks.

The ability of the microcomputer to repeat any particular process or sequence of processes hundreds or thousands of times is particularly important. (The computer, unlike human beings, does not mind doing the same task repeatedly.) It is this ability to repeat sequences of processes that gives computers much of their processing power.

4.4 COMPUTER ANATOMY

Every microcomputer requires specific devices or components to do the inputting, the processing, and the outputting. Therefore, every computer must have at least one input device, a processor device, and an output device.

Input devices include:

- Keyboards
- Joy sticks
- The mouse
- Light pens
- Digitizer tablets
- Disk drives

Output devices include:

- Video display screens
- Printers
- Voice synthesizers
- Device controllers
- Disk drives[1]

The processing unit consists of several devices.[2] These include:

- A *power supply*
- A *"mother board"* (the primary circuit board to which all other circuit boards are connected)
- *Circuit boards* for controlling input and output devices
- *Memory circuit boards*

A microcomputer system may be packaged in a single cabinet (an *integrated system*), which includes the input, processor, and output devices, or it may consist of separate input, output, and processor components hooked together with various cables and connectors (a *component system*). See Figure 4.2. Regardless of the way they are packaged, they operate much the same.

4.5 BITS AND BYTES

The microprocessor consists of many thousands of logic circuits, storage registers, and associated circuits that enable the microcomputer to manipulate and transform

---

[1]Disk drives used for storage and retrieval of data are *both* input and output devices.

[2]On a mainframe computer, the processor device is referred to as the *central processing unit* or simply the "CPU." On a microcomputer, the processor device is called a *microprocessor*.

INTEGRATED SYSTEM

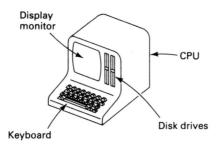

Display
monitor

CPU

Disk drives

Keyboard

COMPONENT SYSTEM

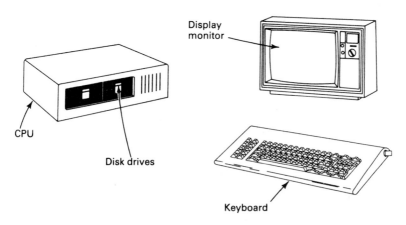

Display
monitor

CPU

Disk drives

Keyboard

Figure 4.2   Microcomputer Systems

data. The logic circuits are programmed to allow current to flow or not to flow. Like an ordinary light switch, they can either be *on* or *off*. (Engineers call such devices two-state or binary devices.) The state of any logic circuit at any particular point in time may be represented as a 1 (one) or 0 (zero), where 1 means *on* and 0 means *off*. Taken by themselves, these ones and zeros mean nothing, but taken in patterns (of say 8 or 16) they can represent a number or a letter of the alphabet.

The binary number system uses combinations of the numerals 1 and 0 to represent any number.[3] For example, 101 in binary represents the decimal number five (4 + 0 + 1 = 5). The decimal number 138 would read 10001010 in binary notation (128 + 0 + 0 + 0 + 8 + 0 + 2 + 0 = 138). Each numeral in a binary number is a *binary digit,* which is usually shortened to *bit* (*bi*nary dig*it*). A bit is one binary digit, a 1 or a 0. Typically, in a microcomputer, bits are arranged in groups or patterns of eight. Each single group of eight bits is called a *byte.*

[3]A brief, non-technical explanation of the binary number system is presented in Appendix A.

A byte (i.e., a group of eight bits) is all that is required to code any selected character. (Characters are numerals, letters of the alphabet, punctuation marks, and special symbols.) This sounds complicated, but it is actually very simple:

$$8 \text{ bits } = 1 \text{ byte } = 1 \text{ character}$$

Why does a microcomputer use eight bits to make up one byte or character code? Why not three or five or ten? To answer this question, it is important to keep in mind that the computer works with binary numbers because zeros and ones conveniently represent two electronic states: on and off. An early concern for computer designers was to develop a code that would economically use as few bits as possible. The problem was to find the least number of bits that it would take to represent all the letters of the alphabet, the numerals, punctuation marks, and other characters that are typically useful. The following chart shows how they tally:

Number of numerals (0 through 9)	= 10
Number of capital letters (A through Z)	= 26
Number of lower case letters (a through z)	= 26
Number of punctuation symbols (,.;:!?/ + -, etc.)	= 32
Total	= 94

The thinking goes something like this: there are 10 numerals, plus 26 capital letters of the alphabet, plus 26 small letters, plus about 32 punctuation marks, and other symbols. This is an approximate total of 94 characters that need to be coded into binary numbers so that the microcomputer can work with them. (This is about the number of characters found on a modern typewriter.) To represent 94 characters in the computer, each *byte* would have to have enough bits to represent a decimal number code at least as big as 94. How many bits does it take?

The maximum number of codes that can be represented by

3 bits	(111) =	8^4
4 bits	(1111) =	16
5 bits	(11111) =	32
6 bits	(111111) =	64
7 bits	(1111111) =	128
8 bits	(11111111) =	256

Anything less than seven bits is too few. Six bits will only allow up to 64 combinations. Seven binary digits will allow 128, more than enough for 94 characters. A computer, then, needs *at least* a seven-bit byte to represent all the needed

[4]The binary number 111 actually represents the number seven (4 + 2 + 1 = 7). The number of codes, however, includes zero, which makes possible, not seven, but eight codes as follows: 000, 001, 010, 011, 100, 101, 110, 111. All ones are shown in the illustration, but all ones in a binary number represent the largest number that can be expressed with a given number of bits.

numbers, letters, and punctuation marks. The number seven, however, is an odd number and a prime number. For this and a few other reasons, seven is not a particularly good number to use. Therefore, most microcomputer designers include one more bit in the group to make an eight-bit byte. (Some microcomputers use only the first seven bits to represent byte codes and ignore the eighth bit or use it for other purposes.)

As it has turned out, having more than 94 codes to work with has been fortuitous. The extra numbers are used for special control signals such as line feeds, carriage returns, tabbing, and other microcomputer operations. Some microcomputers use the extra code numbers above the 128 available for graphic characters or foreign-language characters.

4.6 CODE SCHEMES

Since the microcomputer can only work with binary numbers, a coding scheme has been devised so that different binary numbers represent specific letters and numerals. One coding scheme, ASCII (American Standard for Information Interchange), assigns codes as follows:

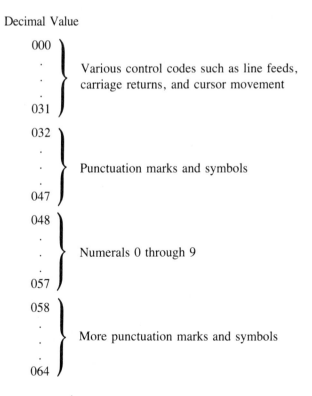

Decimal Value

000
 .
 .
 .   Various control codes such as line feeds,
 .   carriage returns, and cursor movement
031

032
 .
 .   Punctuation marks and symbols
 .
047

048
 .
 .   Numerals 0 through 9
 .
057

058
 .
 .   More punctuation marks and symbols
 .
064

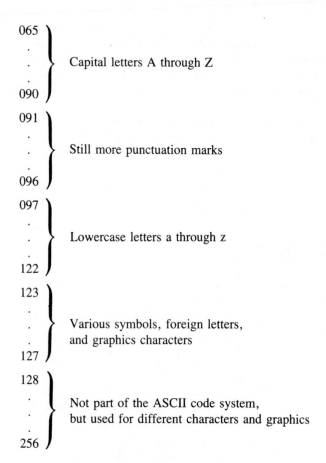

065
.
.
.
090 } Capital letters A through Z

091
.
.
.
096 } Still more punctuation marks

097
.
.
.
122 } Lowercase letters a through z

123
.
.
.
127 } Various symbols, foreign letters, and graphics characters

128
.
.
.
256 } Not part of the ASCII code system, but used for different characters and graphics

For example, the eight-bit binary number

$$01000001$$

is equivalent to the decimal number 65, or the ASCII code for the letter *A*.

Complete words can be represented by a sequence of these numbers. This sequence of the nine numbers, 69 88 69 67 85 84 73 86 69, represents the nine letters E X E C U T I V E, which translates in the microcomputer to EXECUTIVE.

Not all computers use the same character coding scheme. Most microcomputers use the ASCII code system. Other computers (typically mainframe computers) use a different code system, such as the EBCDIC (Extended Binary Coded Decimal Interchange Code) code system, and there are other coding schemes in use. The difference in coding schemes becomes a problem when microcomputers and mainframe computers want to communicate with each other because obviously each system's numbers mean something quite different to the other computer.

4.7 THANKS FOR THE (COMPUTER) MEMORY

RAM, ROM, floppy disk, hard disk, and other terms are used to describe different types of microcomputer memory and data-storage devices. Although there are different devices for storing data in a computer, there are only two basic types of memory, *temporary data memory* and *permanent data memory* (see Figure 4.3). Temporary data memory is also referred to as *internal memory* or *working memory,* or more popularly RAM (random access memory). RAM is our first concern.

Memory Type	Other Terms	Devices
Temporary	RAM Working memory Volatile memory Internal memory	RAM "chips"
Permanent	ROM Disk memory External memory	ROM "chips" or cartridge Hard disk or Fixed disk or Winchester drive Bubble memory

FIGURE 4.3   Types of Memory

4.8 RANDOM-ACCESS MEMORY

A microcomputer's working memory is contained in memory circuit chips. The memory chips are designed so that they can temporarily store the bit codes that represent characters. Chips are grouped so that they will hold several thousand (typically 64,000) bytes or characters. Each byte of memory has a particular *address*. This addressing scheme makes it possible for the microcomputer to locate a particular byte and retrieve its numerical code contents.

The particular combination of ones and zeros in a byte determines the *content* of that byte. As long as the particular combination of numbers does not change, the code number of the character is stored just as if it were written on a piece of paper and stuck in a drawer. This is how the microcomputer "remembers." This is the computer's memory. A microcomputer *stores* information in memory by writing a specific code number at a specific memory address location and then reading the same address location at a later time to see what number was stored there earlier.

Each byte can store the binary code for just one character. Accordingly, it takes a lot of bytes to store anything very extensive. (This sentence is 70 characters long, so it takes 70 bytes to store it.)[5]

While the business of coding and storing each and every separate character in a memory location may appear to be a rather tedious and slow process, actually it happens quite fast. The computer can write information into or read information out of each memory location thousands of times per second.

RAM stores data for several different uses. It stores the programs (instructions) the microcomputer needs for doing certain tasks. It is used to store the data that are currently being worked on by the microprocessor. It stores the data sent to the microprocessor from the keyboard. And it stores the data that have been created by the microprocessor and are waiting to be displayed on the screen.

4.9 RAM CAPACITY

The internal storage capacity of a microcomputer varies widely. Since it takes one byte of storage for each character, it obviously takes a sizable number of such bytes to store and process anything very significant. But how much is enough? It is difficult to imagine how many bytes of memory might be needed for any given computing job, but consider the following. A *full* typewritten page takes up about 4,000 characters of storage space (bytes) as outlined:

Page size: $8^{1}/_{2}$ x 11 in.

Total number of lines:	66	(6 per inch)
Top and bottom margins:	-10	(5 lines each)
	56	
Usable lines per page:	55	
Characters per line:	x72	(average)
Characters per page:	3,960	(average)

Of course, a page that is double-spaced or uses less than 72 characters per line has fewer characters and therefore takes up less space in memory.

---

[5]This explanation is a simplification of how such data are stored, but it is conceptually accurate. The actual, physical storage of data bits is somewhat more technical and beyond the scope of this book.

Computer memory is measured in units of thousands of bytes (kilobytes or K bytes) and in units of millions of bytes (megabytes or M bytes). For convenience, computer memory is expressed as a binary multiple such as 4K, 16K, 32K, 64K, 128K, 256K, 512K, and so on. These numbers represent a rounded value of the true number of bytes available. The amount of memory referred to as 64K of memory is actually 65,536 bytes. Use of the rounded numbers is just an easy way of remembering and referring to memory sizes.

How much is enough? The complexity of work that can be done by a microcomputer and the amount of data that can be processed in a given amount of time are determined to a large extent by the amount of RAM memory that is available to the microprocessor. Some microcomputers operate with very limited memory, and their capability is accordingly very restricted. As microcomputers are called on to run programs that are more complex and sophisticated, they require more internal memory. Most microcomputers allow for the expansion of memory capacity just by the installation of a circuit board that holds additional RAM chips.

While few microcomputers are sold with less than 64 K bytes of internal (working) memory, a microcomputer intended for serious business use should have more—much more. Many programs currently available require between 128K and 196K bytes to work at all. For sophisticated business use, 256K is about the minimum. Although some users see no need to have such large amounts of memory, the addition of RAM is one of the first enhancements sought by serious microcomputer users. Companies purchasing new microcomputers should consider purchasing adequate memory capacity at the time of the original purchase.

When it comes to microcomputer memory, more is definitely better. It should be noted, though, that RAM memory is not infinitely expandable. The design of the microprocessor itself sets limitations on the amount of internal or working memory that can be addressed and therefore used by the microcomputer.

4.10 PERMANENT DATA STORAGE

RAM can store data only while the microcomputer power is turned on and the microcomputer is active. Once the power is turned off (powered down), the RAM can no longer sustain its memory states and all temporarily stored data disappear. Each time the microcomputer is turned off, the internally stored programs and data are lost. That is why it is also necessary to have *permanent storage devices*. Each time the microcomputer is turned back on (powered up), program data must be loaded into RAM memory once again.

A microcomputer would be impossibly difficult to use if each time it was turned on the programs and data had to be entered again character by character from the keyboard. Fortunately, permanent memory devices make it possible for data and programs to be saved on disk files and then easily loaded back into the internal memory (RAM) whenever needed. Devices for saving programs and data files are generically called *mass storage devices* (because they store massive amounts of data), but they are more popularly known by such names as as *floppy disks* and *hard disks*.

4.11 READ-ONLY MEMORY

Read-only memory (ROM) is a special memory circuit chip that has been loaded with a program or data at the factory. Data cannot be "written" to a ROM, but only "read" from it. ROM chips are a necessary component in most microcomputers. They provide special data and programs required for the operation of the computer. ROMs are used in most microcomputers to help start it up when the microcomputer is first turned on and to provide the special operating instructions required by the microcomputer.

Removable ROM cartridges containing program software are also sold for some microcomputers, particularly small portables. The ROM cartridge is plugged into a special connector slot on the microcomputer and provides access to stored programs in the same way as the floppy disk, except that programs and data cannot be saved to the ROM since a ROM is a *read-only* device.

4.12 FLOPPY DISKS

Floppy disks are the most popular form of permanent data storage for microcomputers. The terms *floppy, disk,* and *diskette* all refer to the same thing. A floppy disk consists of a paper thin disk of flexible plastic. This disk is covered with a metallic oxide coating that can be readily magnetized. This flexible, circular disk is permanently enclosed in a square envelope of durable black plastic to protect it and to aid in handling. (Figure 4.4) An oval window in the square envelope allows the disk read/write heads to contact the magnetic surface. As the disk spins in the drive, the read/write head moves radially aross its surface, much in the fashion of a phonograph.

As the disk rotates, the head writes (i.e. records) very small *blips* of magnetism on the surface, Magnetized in one direction, the blip becomes a data bit 0, and magnetized in the other direction, the blip becomes a 1. Once written to the disk, these data bits can be read back from the disk. They remain there more or less permanently until erased or inadvertently destroyed.

Even though disks are ruggedly designed for everyday use and handling, some care must be exercised in their use. The magnetic coating can be damaged, and once damaged, all data stored on that spot (and perhaps the whole disk) is lost.

Any area of the disk not covered by the protective envelope is at risk. The area in the read/write window especially exposes the magnetic surface to all sorts of hazards such as finger prints, cigarette smoke and ashes, airborne dust, coffee spills, and the like. The most tiny particle or scratch can permanently damage a disk. For this reason, the disk should never be picked up or handled in such a manner that fingers touch the exposed areas of the disk surface itself. Likewise,

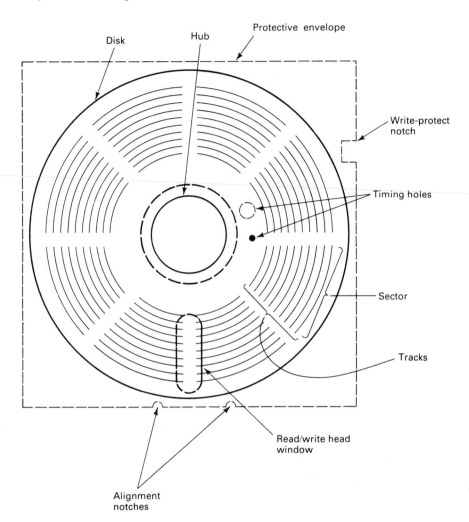

Figure 4.4   Floppy Diskette (5 1/4 inch)

nothing should be allowed to contact the exposed area. The disk should not be stored or used in other than normal room temperatures, and it must be kept away from stray sources of magnetism such as electric motors, magnets, and electronic devices.

Floppy disks come in 8-, 5 1/4, and 3 1/2-in. sizes. The 5 1/4-in. size is the most prevalent and comes the closest to becoming the standard for microcomputers.

Floppy disks differ greatly in the amount of data they can store and in the *formats* in which they store it. Some floppy disk units use both sides of a disk (double sided) whereas other units use only one side (single-sided). Because it is using both sides of the disk, a double-sided disk will store twice as much data as a single-sided disk. Since double-sided drives give twice the data storage, they are preferable to single sided drives, and they cost very little more. A single-sided floppy disk drive will not read a double-sided disk, although a double-sided drive unit will usually read a single-sided disk.

4.13 DISK FORMATTING

The disk drive writes the data on the disk in a special pattern called a *format* so that it knows where to look for data the next time it is read. Although you cannot tell the disk's format by just looking at the disk, it must be recorded there magnetically before the microcomputer will operate properly.

A disk is formatted into wedge-shaped segments called *sectors*, and then each sector is divided into concentric *tracks*. The microcomputer assigns data to specific locations on a disk by writing it to a specific sector and track address. The addresses of specific files of data are stored in a designated area of the disk (usually the first one or two tracks) called the disk *directory*. This is all done automatically by a special formatting program in the microcomputer, which the user runs with each new disk. The formatting program also sets up a directory for that particular disk. The directory of any disk can then be displayed at any time so that the user can see what data files are stored on that disk.

The way in which the data are arranged on a disk (the way in which data are *formatted*) varies from manufacturer to manufacturer. Floppy disks vary with respect to the number of sectors and tracks in their formats. There is no official standard. A disk formatted on one microcomputer usually cannot be read by a microcomputer produced by another manufacturer *unless the manufacturer has purposefully designed the microcomputer to be compatible.*[6]

Floppy disk systems are an excellent answer to the need for permanent data storage. They are very inexpensive, highly reliable, and are "removable media," which means each disk can be removed from the microcomputer and stored anywhere else. Floppy disks also have the advantage that they can be easily mailed to other users.

4.14 HARD DISKS

Hard-disk permanent data storage devices (also called *fixed disks*) are similar to floppy disk storage devices except that the disk itself is made of a rigid material and the disk is enclosed in a sealed drive unit that operates with a much higher degree of precision. This precision makes it possible to store a greater amount of

---

[6]Although no official standard exists, the popularity of the IBM-PC has created a very large pool of commercially available software. The availability of this software has, in turn, encouraged manufacturers to create microcomputers that could read the disks on which these programs were furnished. The IBM-PC disk configuration, then, has become a *de facto* standard simply because so many manufacturers have chosen to abide by it.

data on a given surface area and to read and write data much faster. The hard disk is a completely enclosed device. Its disks are not removable, but it can store 30 to 50 times more data than an equivalent sized floppy. For users who require very rapid access to large amounts of data (and most business users soon have that requirement), the hard disk drive is an excellent choice for mass data storage.

Recent technology has produced a *removable* hard disk system. This system combines the advantages of hard disk systems with the advantages of the removable floppy disk systems. The disks store large quantities of data (typically 10 megabytes per disk), but the hard disk can be removed and replaced with a new, empty disk or a disk containing another previously stored set of data.

4.15 DATA STORAGE CAPACITIES

The data storage capacity of floppy disk and hard disk systems varies greatly. The earliest microcomputer systems stored barely more than 100,000 bytes on a disk. New systems make it possible to store more than 1 million bytes in the same area, and it is to be expected that storage densities will steadily increase over the next several years.

The storage capacity for any system varies from manufacturer to manufacturer. Users should be aware that not all the rated storage capacity on each floppy is actually available for use by the user, as some space is taken up by the disk's directory and other necessary system files.

While the storage capacity of a single floppy disk ranges from 100K bytes to more than 1 megabyte (typically 360K bytes), once a floppy disk is full, you can remove it and put in another blank disk. Used in this fashion, the storage capacity of a floppy disk system is infinitely expandable by simply adding new, very inexpensive floppy disks.

However, one of the chief disadvantages of floppy disks is the problem of keeping track of what data and program files are on what disk and making sure the correct disk is in the disk drive when it is needed. It takes a surprisingly short time to accumulate hundreds of such files. A floppy disk system tends not to work well if a given program requires frequent "swapping" of disks in and out of the disk drives because the data are contained on several different disks.

The solution to this particular problem is the hard disk system. Hard disk storage systems have a fixed amount of storage space (except for the new, removable hard disk systems), but the memory capacity is much greater than on a single floppy disk. With a hard disk system, any file of data is always instantly available. Capacities of hard disk drives are usually 5, 10, 20, and 40 megabytes and greater. The cost of hard disk systems is also greater than for floppy disk systems, but the price differential (on a unit cost per storage unit basis) is shrinking rapidly.

How much storage capacity should a business system possess? It depends. The utility of having permanent storage capacity for a single microcomputer system beyond about 20 megabytes becomes questionable. A 20-megabyte system holds between 5,000 and 10,000 pages of text, data, or programs (depending on the number of characters per page). Amounts of data of that magnitude are seldom the exclusive domain of a single user. When data files exist that contain these amounts, they usually require access by other users, access by data entry clerks, and the like. Computing jobs requiring greater capacity may more properly belong on a multiuser microcomputer system, a local area network of microcomputers, or perhaps a minicomputer or mainframe computer system.

4.16 WHEN IS A MICROCOMPUTER NO LONGER A MICROCOMPUTER?

The short history of microcomputer hardware is characterized by rapid change in capability and capacity. The original microcomputers all used eight-bit microprocessors (were able to process only eight bits of information at the same time). Sixteen-bit microprocessors are now more common, and some microcomputers are using thirty-two bit microprocessors. Each of these new generations of microprocessors significantly increases the speed and memory capacity of the microcomputers in which they are used.

Microcomputer technology has grown to the point where the functional capabilities (not necessarily the processing capabilities) rival those of mainframe computers for dedicated, single-purpose uses.

As microcomputers continue to grow in functional capability, and particularly as they are linked into local area networks and mainframe networks of multiple users accessing centralized databases, they begin to lose their strict identity as microcomputers. The differences that at one time clearly distinguished microcomputers from minicomputer and mainframe computer systems are rapidly blurring.

5

Something About Software

All computers, including microcomputers, are basically dumb. They have no motives and they do not act on their own volition. They do only what they are constructed and instructed to do. They can only carry out the activities programmed into them by human engineers, programmers, and users.

Sometimes computers seem very smart because they can add, subtract, multiply, and divide and move data around very fast and with great precision, things we humans do extremely slowly by comparison. They seem clever because we ask them questions and they can provide us with complex answers in a brief span of time. But the machine itself, although extremely fast in moving its electronic gears, is only displaying and carrying out the cleverness of its engineers and those who direct its every move—the programmers.

5.1 MAKING THE DUMB MACHINE WORK

A computer cannot do anything without being told very specifically and in great detail what to do. The instructions telling a computer what to do must be written in a language or set of coded instructions that the computer understands and which the machine can then execute one at a time in sequence. Whole sets of such instructions make up what we call *computer programs*. Programs are collectively called *software* to distinguish them from the machine or equipment parts, which are referred to as *hardware*. Programs may do simple tasks like adding a column of numbers, or they may do complex operations such as the general accounting for a large company.

5.2 SOFTWARE

Because a computer system is totally dependent on the instructions that are programmed into it, one of the most critical parts of any computer system is the software that makes it work. The software is most important because it alone is what tells the computer to carry out useful processes. It provides the link between the conceptual needs of human users and the physical electrons that ultimately do the work. Without programs, a microcomputer would just be an idle collection of electronic parts. To the computer user, programs are vitally important.

Although simple microcomputer programs can be designed in minutes, programs that do really useful work in a business environment are complex and take months to design, code, and test. Much of the development time is spent making sure that the program will work right every time and be free of *most* errors or *bugs* (although even with the most professional, conscientious effort, virtually all complex computer programs have a few lingering bugs that eventually make themselves known to users).

5.3 MICROCOMPUTER LANGUAGES

A digital computer can only work with binary numbers. Therefore, instructions given to a computer must at some point be given as a sequence of binary numbers. While it is possible to write a microcomputer program using binary numbers, the tedium and complexity of working with long strings of ones and zeros makes that task exceedingly difficult, if not impossible for most of us.

Fortunately, there is another solution. Rather than write programs in binary number sequences, other languages have been developed that use word commands in place of ones and zeros. These word languages make programming a microcomputer (or any computer) far easier.

While the microcomputer works with its "native" (binary number system) language, we human beings work best with a language that is closer to our native language. Special computer programs have been designed that make it possible for the programmer to write instructions in an English-like language. These instructions are then translated by the microcomputer into the binary numbers readily understood by the computer.

A few of the most widely used languages implemented on microcomputers are:

- Assembler
- BASIC
- FORTRAN
- COBOL
- Pascal
- C

Assembler is considered to be a *low-level* language. This means that it is not very English-like. It uses mnemonics such as *mov, jmp, ret, push,* and *pop* and hexadecimal (base 16) numbers to instruct the computer. Assembler is easier than programming with binary numbers, but it is still a very complex and difficult language to use. It is primarily a language for professional programmers. Assembler's chief advantage is that it translates into very efficient binary sequences, and therefore programs run very fast and efficiently.

5.4 HIGH-LEVEL LANGUAGES

BASIC is the most widely known and widely used microcomputer language.[1] Its popularity stems from the fact that it is easy to learn. BASIC was devised originally as a beginner's language to ease students into programming.[2] The acronym BASIC stands for *B*eginners *A*ll-purpose *S*ymbolic *I*nstruction *C*ode. The language's authors chose existing English words for BASIC's commands, as these two program examples illustrate.

BASIC Program (Example A)

```
10  PRINT "Enter your name: ";
20  INPUT YOURNAME$
30  PRINT "Your name is "; YOURNAME$
40  END
```

[1]Some programmers would argue that, although BASIC is the most *used* microcomputer language, it is not necessarily the best. Recently developed computer languages, like Pascal, help eliminate errors and prolonged testing because they force the programmer to structure programs more carefully. Efforts are underway, however, to make BASIC a more structured language, which would lessen these objections.

[2]The BASIC computer language was created at Dartmouth College by John Kemeny and Thomas Kurtz.

BASIC Program (Example B)

```
10 PRINT "Enter a number: ";
20 INPUT FIRSTNUMBER
30 PRINT "Enter another number: ";
40 INPUT SECONDNUMBER
50 LET PRODUCT = FIRSTNUMBER * SECONDNUMBER
60 PRINT "The product of these two numbers is "; PRODUCT
70 END
```

A BASIC program consists of a separate command on each line. Each line starts with a line number. Each command keyword is printed in all capital letters. The command PRINT tells the computer to display something on the screen. The command INPUT tells the microcomputer to accept data typed in at the keyboard.

How does the program work? Let us look at Example Program A line by line. Line 10 in Example Program A tells the microcomputer to "prompt" the user to type in his or her name by printing (on the video display screen) the message "Enter your name: ". Line 20 tells the microcomputer to receive data entered at the keyboard and store it in a *variable* with the declared name of YOURNAME$. A variable is a memory storage location. (YOURNAME$ is simply a designated place in memory where data can be temporarily stored.) Line 30 then tells the microcomputer to print the message "Your name is " followed by what has previously been stored in the variable YOURNAME$. The last line tells the microcomputer that it has reached the end of the program.

Program B functions in a similar manner except that numbers rather than names are processed. Line 10 tells the microcomputer to print (again on the video display screen) the message "Enter a number: ". Line 20 tells it to receive data input at the keyboard and store it in the variable FIRSTNUMBER. Line 30 tells it to print a second message, "Enter another number: ". Line 40 tells it to receive new data and store it in a variable called SECONDNUMBER. Line 50 tells the microcomputer to let a third variable, PRODUCT, contain the results of the computation, where the contents of the variable FIRSTNUMBER are multiplied by the contents of the variable SECONDNUMBER. (The * symbol is used to indicate multiplication.) Line 60 tells the microcomputer to display the message "The product of these two numbers is ", followed by what is now the calculated contents of the variable PRODUCT. Line 70, of course, indicates the end of this program.

BASIC is fairly easy to learn. Although it started out as a fairly simple, rudimentary language, it has "grown up" over the years. Now, with many enhancements and added commands in recent versions, it has become a sophisticated and powerful language, especially for noncomputer professionals and microcomputer users in particular. While it is not a perfect language (there is no perfect language), it will no doubt continue to be popular for a number of years.

FORTRAN is one of the oldest computer languages still in use. Its name stands for *for*mula *tran*slation. It was originally designed for scientific and mathematic applications and still has a large following of programmers in engineering, mathematics, and science.

COBOL (*CO*mmon *B*usiness-*O*riented *L*anguage) is principally a language for mainframes. It was designed for business applications that require extensive file handling. Although many programs already written in COBOL would be useful to run on microcomputers, programs written in COBOL require a large amount of RAM and data storage, and because they were originally written for mainframe systems, they to tend not to run well on microcomputers. As new COBOL compilers are developed, however, this may change.

Pascal (named in honor of Blaise Pascal) is one of a new generation of languages. It is a very concise and tightly structured language. The structured quality helps programmers avoid many of the programming errors that are easily made in other languages. Pascal has become especially popular with microcomputer programmers.

The C language is also a new generation programming language that is gaining in popularity by microcomputer programmers. C is a high-level language that produces very compact programs that run very fast and efficiently. In many respects, C has many of the advantages of Assembler, but is far less difficult to learn and use. The major advantage of C is that the same source program, once written, can be compiled and run on many different makes and models of microcomputers (at least all of those for which a C compiler has been written). In the parlance of microcomputer program designers, C is *portable*. Despite its advantages, C is a professional programmer's language. It is not likely to be used by the beginning programmer.

In the corporate environment, most programs will be obtained through commercial sources. In this case, the language used will be of little consequence so long as the program functions as it is supposed to function. In a few cases, however, programs will be written by the user, or perhaps by a paid professional programmer.[3]

When business users want to write programs for their own use, they will likely use BASIC simply because it is easy to learn and once learned is not soon forgotten. Professional programmers or those who have advanced programming skills will likely choose BASIC, Assembler, Pascal, or C.

Another newer class of programming languages must be mentioned. They are recently created languages for data-base management systems and are collectively called *fourth-generation languages*. They are also sometimes referred to as *non-procedural languages*, although this is confusing since specific programs (procedures) can be written using them. These languages provide simple, but powerful commands that enable users to write complex programs for storing and retrieving data in database systems. These languages are very English-like and are therefore relatively easy to learn, yet they allow users to write programs that previously could only be developed by professional programmers. As database management systems come into common use, it is to be expected that more and more users will write their own programs using these languages.

---

[3]Some data-processing departments have programmers assigned exclusively to programming for microcomputers.

5.5 COMPILED AND INTERPRETED CODE

Any microcomputer using a program written in a language other than binary must translate the program statements into binary numbers before they can be executed by the computer. This translation is done in one of two ways, either by *interpreting* or by *compiling*. The first method, interpreting, requires that each individual line of instruction be translated by the computer and then executed. The first line is translated, then executed. The second line is translated, then executed, and then the next line, the next, and so on, until all lines have been successively translated and executed.

The second method, compiling, requires that all lines of instruction be first translated into machine language and then saved in a separate, new file. This new file, consisting only of binary numbers is then read into the microcomputer for execution. When a program is compiled, a new set of command statements *in machine language* is created. The original version is called the *source code*. The resulting machine-language version after compiling is called *object code*. The special program that makes the translation is called the *compiler*.

Interpreted programs and compiled programs each have their pros and cons. Because each statement must be translated before being executed, interpreted programs run much slower than compiled programs. The chief advantage of interpreted programs is that during program development a few lines of coded instruction can be written, the program can be run, and, if there is an error, it can be quickly found and fixed.

Finding and correcting errors in interpreted programs is usually much faster than finding and correcting errors in compiled programs. Correcting compiled programs requires finding the error in the source code, changing the source code, and then recompiling the revised version into new object code. The chief advantage of compiled programs is that, because they have already been converted to binary numbers, they run faster. They also may make more efficient use of memory.

Microcomputer programs may be of either type—compiled or interpreted. Commercially distributed software is usually compiled because it runs faster and uses memory more efficiently, and because the code cannot be easily deciphered. Most user-developed programs in BASIC are interpreted programs because they are easier to develop and require less knowledge and skill on the part of the programmer. They can also be executed immediately without waiting for the code to compile.

5.6 OPERATING SYSTEMS

Every microcomputer has a special program that controls what is done during every microsecond the microcomputer is in operation. This program, called the *operating system,* is like a traffic cop directing various bits of information to where they should go and in what order. The operating system coordinates the work of the microcomputer by telling it when it should accept information from the keyboard, where it should store information, and how it should do certain kinds of operations and hundreds of other important duties. Microcomputer systems that use disk drives (and almost all do) require additional program instructions to coordinate disk access. These systems have an operating system called the *disk operating system,* or, more familiarly, DOS.

When the microcomputer is first turned on, it must have a small program to tell itself how to get started. There is a small program in ROM memory that tells the microcomputer just that—how to get itself started. This program is called the *boot* or *bootstrap* program because it helps the microcomputer "pull itself up by its bootstraps." The boot program brings the microcomputer up to operating status by first loading the operating system into memory. The DOS (disk operating system) then allows the user to load and run other programs.

Programs that are compiled into machine language can be run directly from DOS. The user usually just types in the program's name and it begins running. BASIC language programs that are to be interpreted require that the user first load the BASIC interpreter program. Once BASIC has been loaded into memory, the user can then load and run a program written in BASIC.

As Figure 5.1 shows, microcomputer programs exist at various levels. Programs written in BASIC (interpreted BASIC) are run only within the BASIC interpreter program. The BASIC interpreter program itself runs only within the DOS (disk operating system) program. Machine-language (compiled) programs also run within DOS.

Most microcomputers are intended to be used by a single user doing one job at a time. The operating system is therefore designed to support only this one user. Some microcomputers, however, have enough computing power that they can serve several users at one time (where each user works on a separate *terminal* connected

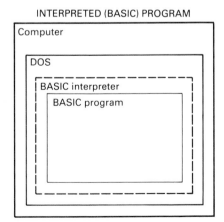

Figure 5.1   Levels of Programs: Compiled and Interpreted

to the microcomputer). Alternatively, one user can have several computing jobs (tasks) going at the same time, such as printing one document while another is being edited. Microcomputer systems capable of serving several users at the same time or doing multiple tasks at the same time are called *multiuser* and *multitasking* microcomputers. These microcomputer systems require special operating systems that support multiuser and multitasking operations.

5.7 APPLICATION PROGRAMS

Programs like DOS and BASIC are *systems* programs. They provide the underlying system to help other programs execute properly. The other programs, which do specific jobs for microcomputer users, such as accounting programs, financial management, word processing, business graphics, and the like, are called *application programs*. Application programs are the programs that do the real-world computing jobs of interest to business users. Application programs will be discussed in the next few chapters.

CHAPTER

6

Uses of the Microcomputer

A microcomputer, *like the human mind,* is a processor of numbers, words, and images. Indeed, a microcomputer is an *extension of the human mind* in the same sense that a hammer is an extension of the human hand, the telephone is an extension of our hearing, or a book is an extension of our memory. The computer allows the human mind to amplify its ability to store and retrieve information, to manipulate numbers and symbols, to write, to draw, and to communicate ideas in a variety of forms both quickly and flexibly. The microcomputer is a tool for the mind.

6.1 WIZARDRY WITH NUMBERS, WORDS, AND IMAGES

Conceptually, the relationship between a user and a microcomputer is simple. The user puts raw data (numbers, words, and images) into the microcomputer: the microcomputer, in turn, transforms this raw data into a new pattern of information and finally displays this transformed data back to the user. While the relationship between user and microcomputer is conceptually simple, in practice it is highly complex, requiring the use of very sophisticated and very well developed programs. What may appear at times to be sheer wizardry is really the product of thorough systems analysis, creative program design, and carefully crafted program logic. The ability of the microcomputer to do useful work is no accident.

6.2 BUSINESS APPLICATIONS

The number of business applications to which microcomputer technology can be applied is virtually unlimited. If the activity involves working with numbers, formulas, words, reports, charts, graphs—in short, any activity more traditionally using a pencil, typewriter, calculator, or file cabinet—chances are that a microcomputer can do the job faster and better.

What can a microcomputer do? Microcomputers have shown their worth for tasks involving scheduling, PERT and network development, and quality control. They have been applied to activities involving finances, loans, investments, marketing and sales, inventory, facilities and maintenance, manufacturing and production, and personnel. The following list, although by no means comprehensive, suggests some of the applications that have become microcomputer fare.

Financial Management

- General Ledger
- Accounts Receivable
- Sales-order Entry
- Accounts Payable Critical Ratios
- Critical Ratios
- Cash-flow Analysis
- Risk Management
- Return on Investment
- Net Present Value
- Income Statement
- Balance Sheet
- Pro Forma
- Capital Expenditure Analysis
- Budget Preparation
- Budget/Performance Analysis
- Cost-Value-Profit Analysis
- Break-even Analysis
- Planned Expense Analysis
- Price/Cost Ratios
- Benefit/Cost Analysis
- Make-Versus-Buy Analysis
- Lease/Purchase Analysis

- Expense Account Category Analysis
- Cost of Goods Sold
- General and Administrative Expense Analysis
- Depreciation Schedules
- Salvage Value
- Depreciation Amount
- Tax Strategies Analysis

Loan Management

- Maximum Loan Amount
- Mortgage Amortization
- Annual Interest Rate
- Term of a Loan
- Remaining Balance
- Rebate Due
- Regular Payment on a Loan
- Last Payment on a Loan
- Principal on a Loan

Investment Management

- Bond Portfolio Analysis
- Stock Portfolio Analysis
- Nominal Interest Rate on an Investment
- Effective Interest Rate on an Investment
- Earned Interest Tables
- Future Value of an Investment
- Annuity
- Regular Withdrawals
- Initial Investment
- Minimal Investment for Withdrawals

Marketing and Sales Management

- Market Forecasting
- Pricing Analysis
- Retail Markup
- Sales Versus Overhead
- Sales Commissions

- Sales Summaries
- Market Variance Analysis
- Projected Versus Actual Performance Analysis
- Top-product Analysis
- Profitability Forecasting
- Seasonal Index
- Mailing-list-quality Analysis
- Advertising Cost Analysis
- Market Strategy Performance Analysis
- Catalog Production Scheduling
- Market Survey Analysis
- Customer Preference Analysis
- Mail-order Sales Analysis
- Seasonal Sales Forecasting
- Order Tracking
- Time-in-transit Analysis
- Shipping Method Analysis
- Shipping Container Size Optimization Analysis
- Selling Expense Analysis
- Price Quotes
- Sales Contracts

Inventory Management

- Economic Order Quantity
- End-of-year Inventory Estimates
- Value of Inventory
- In-stock Position
- Stock Turnaround Analysis
- Distribution Analysis
- Warehouse Space Use Analysis
- Warehouse Growth Forecasting

Facilities and Maintenance Management

- Resource Allocation
- Utilization Rates
- Operational Availability
- Mean Maintenance Down Time

- Mean Time between Failures
- Inherent/Achieved Availability
- Mean Preventive Maintenance Time
- Mean Active Maintenance Time
- Mean Time between Maintenance
- Preventive Maintenance Scheduling
- Life-cycle Costs
- Route Analysis

Manufacturing and Production Management

- Material-yield Analysis
- Payoff Analysis
- Production Planning
- Product Cost Analysis
- Seasonal Product Manufacturing Forecasting

Personnel Management

- Payroll
- EEO Analysis
- Salary Analysis
- Benefits Analysis
- Incentive Plan Forecasting
- Productivity Analysis
- Performance Evaluation
- Absence/Sickleave Analysis
- Recreational Facility Reservation Scheduling
- Training

Miscellaneous

- Daily Expense Log
- Professional Fee Calculation
- Project Cost Estimating
- Project Scheduling
- Project Staffing Analysis
- Policy and Procedures Management
- Organizational Charts

- Presentation Graphics
- Alphabetizing/Sorting Lists
- Days between Two Dates
- Systems Documentation
- Hardware/Software Requirements Forecasting

This list represents the kind of business activities that have been found to be usefully supported by microcomputer technology. In almost every example, the application involves quantitative manipulation—working with numerical data. Modern management practices tend to place an emphasis on quantitative techniques involving statistics, probabilities, scheduling, financial modeling, and numerical analysis. Microcomputers seem to be made for such tasks.

6.3 GENERIC APPLICATIONS PROGRAMS

The earliest programs written for microcomputers were single minded in the sense that they focused primarily on doing just number processing or just word processing or (somewhat later) just graphics. Applications involving the processing of these three—numbers, words, and images—were termed *generic applications*. Even though there is considerable integration of these three processes in today's increasingly sophisticated microcomputer software programs, single-purpose programs still abound.

In addition to the processing of numbers, words, and graphic images, two other generic applications must be added. These are *data storage and retrieval programs* and *data-communications programs*. The full complement of generic programs, then, is the three symbol-processing functions—numbers, words, and graphic images—plus data storage and retrieval and data communications. It is helpful to think of data storage and retrieval as microcomputing processes that extend over *time* (i.e., data are stored at one time for retrieval at a later time) and data communications as microcomputing processes that extend over *distance* (i.e., data are sent and received between interconnected computers).

Every application of microcomputer technology is in some sense a specialized application, but the use of generic categories is useful as a means of gaining broad familiarity with typical microcomputer applications. We begin our survey of these generic applications by looking first at number processing.

CHAPTER
7

Working
with Numbers

The first mainframe computers were designed solely for the purpose of processing numbers, and even today the very largest computer systems are used primarily for processing numerical data. The processing of numbers is something that computers can do very well. Microcomputers, provided that the volume of data does not get too extensive, can also do a very creditable job with numbers.

7.1 CRUNCHING NUMBERS

Business is inherently a numbers game. A large percentage of business operations can be described mathematically. Many formulas and models have been created to assist managers to describe or project business activities. The information derived from the use of such formulas and models serves the continuous stream of management decision processes. The current crop of number-processing programs for business falls loosely into the following categories.

- Spreadsheet Calculations
- Financial Management

- Forecasting
- Accounting
- Inventory Management
- Statistics
- Income Tax Preparation
- Cost Analysis
- Budgeting
- Stock Market Projections and Tracking
- Property Management
- Banking and Loan Calculations
- Laboratory Measurements

Commercial programs are not available for some of the applications listed. Many programs have been created by users for their own use. This does not mean that most business users are faced with the prospect of writing their own microcomputer programs. The number and variety of business applications programs grows daily, but the electronic spreadsheet is a very quick way of creating one's own numerical applications software.

7.2 ELECTRONIC SPREADSHEET PROGRAMS

The single, most outstanding microcomputer program is the electronic spreadsheet. It has fired the enthusiasm of serious business users since it was first introduced. Some say that this program alone sparked the microcomputer revolution. Certainly, it has had an enormous stimulating effect on business microcomputing. In 1978, two bright and enterprising fellows, Dan Bricklin and Bob Frankston, created and marketed a spread-sheet program for microcomputers, which they called VISICALC[1] This extremely useful program has enjoyed a great and well-deserved popularity. Although VISICALC is perhaps the best-known program of its type, there have been more than 50 other microcomputer software companies who have marketed similar spreadsheet programs.

Exactly what is an electronic spreadsheet? The simplest description of an electronic spreadsheet program is that it is a sophisticated numerical calculator. But truly it is much more than that. When the spreadsheet program is initiated, the microcomputer displays a worksheet of columns and rows much as you would see on a blank ledger sheet or columnar pad. The columns are labeled with letters (A, B, C, etc.) up to about 64 columns. The rows are similarly labeled (1, 2, 3, etc.) up to about 256 rows. The potential spreadsheet size is very large. (Some spreadsheet programs have virtually unlimited size).

---

[1]VISICALC is a registered trademark of VisiCorp, Inc.

Of course, not all 64 columns and 256 rows show on the screen at one time. Only a selected rectangular area of the total spreadsheet is in view at one time, but the user can press cursor keys that scroll the screen up or down, left or right bringing different sections of a larger work area into view.

The intersection of any particular column and row coordinate is called a *cell*. The cell or coordinate of column A and row 1 is, logically, A1. Going *across* the first spreadsheet row, cells are labeled A1, B1, C1, and so on. Going *down* the first spreadsheet column, cells are labeled A1, A2, A3, and so on.

Within any spreadsheet cell, the user can enter *either* numbers or words. The numbers can be either a specific number value or a formula for calculating some needed value from values given in other cells. Label information can be a single letter, a word, or a short phrase.

A spreadsheet program can be used just as one would use a ledger sheet. For instance, in preparing a budget, (see Figure 7.1), the categories (labels) of expenditures could be listed, say, in column A. Then, for each expenditure categorized, an amount could be listed, say, in column C.

With an electronic spreadsheet, it is a simple thing to calculate subtotals, totals, and other statistics and values for different categories. The ability to work with formulas gives an electronic spreadsheet its enormous power. Formulas may be placed in any cell where the answer to the formula is to appear. The variables in the formula itself may refer to the values contained in any other cell. When the formula is calculated, it looks to see what value is currently in the cells that are referenced by the formula so that the calculation is always done using the most

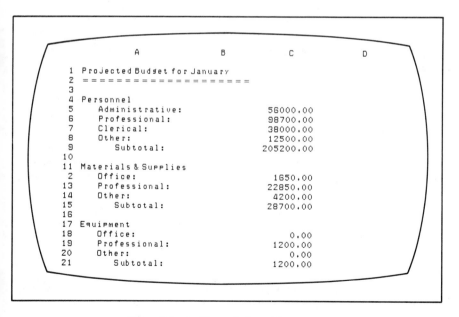

Figure 7.1   An Electronic Spreadsheet

recently entered data values. It is possible to set up relationships between cell values (i.e., to create a *model*) describing how the totals and subtotals are to be calculated, and then to enter data in the appropriate cells and let the spreadsheet do all the calculations instantly and automatically. The electronic spreadsheet will perform calculations very quickly on demand. New values can be reentered easily and recalculations are accomplished at the press of a key.

The utility of an electronic spreadsheet becomes quickly apparent when many different values need to be calculated using the same set of formulas or data relationships. For example, a monthly budget may use the same formulas and, by merely substituting the values for each month in turn, separate budget spreadsheets can quickly be generated. Any value changes can easily be accomplished with the stroke of a few keys. By substituting a new value for an old value, it is possible to calculate quick answers for changing cost rates, discounts, overhead rates, tax percentages, break-evens, amortizations, and all sorts of business formulas.

The most exciting use of the electronic spreadsheet has been for "what if . . . " analysis. The spreadsheet lends itself to entering different data based on projected or hypothetical conditions that may affect business strategies and planning. For example, a market strategist may wish to produce several sets of projections based on varying assumptions about the economy, marketing costs, and projected sales. The production of such reports by hand might easily consume several days' effort. With an electronic spreadsheet, such reports can be generated in a few hours, perhaps even minutes.

Electronic spreadsheet programs are ideal for developing budgets, creating pricing models, calculating break-even points, preparing cash-flow analyses, creating investment models, managing portfolios, preparing net worth and profit and loss statements, and many other calculation problems that require a high degree of user judgment and interaction. Some programs have built-in functions that allow the automatic calculation of statistics (sums, frequency counts, averages, standard deviations, and net present value).

Like most other microcomputer programs, spread-sheet programs have been improved over time. The newer, more sophisticated electronic spreadsheets provide greater size (more columns and rows), allow more formatting options, and feature more statistical functions.

A spreadsheet is fundamentally a two-dimensional (column/row) workspace, but newer versions go beyond two dimensions. These spreadsheets allow the user to place into a cell a reference to another cell in another spreadsheet. (The other spreadsheet must be available on the disk.) This makes it possible for the user to work in three dimensions at the same time. For example, a spreadsheet might be created to summarize budget expenditures over a whole year. If a separate spreadsheet were kept for each calendar month, then an end-of-year summary spreadsheet could be prepared just by referencing appropriate cells in 12 previously created monthly spreadsheets.

Other spreadsheet features permit the user to write separate procedural programs and to call those programs from a cell. This makes it possible for the spreadsheet to use not only formulas, but the results of completely separate microcomputer programs. Still other features permit the user to display the results of spreadsheet calculations graphically.

The electronic spreadsheet is one of the most valuable tools for financial management and planning. There is simply no other tool like it, and its capabilities are only beginning to be tapped.

7.3 ACCOUNTING PROGRAMS

In larger companies, the accounting function has traditionally been the prerogative of the data-processing department using mainframe computers. Because of the massive volume of data that must be processed for large corporations and for reasons relating to data integrity and security, the accounting function will undoubtedly stay there. However, many small businesses (particularly those that are just beginning to automate their accounting function) are finding the microcomputer to be both an affordable and sensible way to meet their accounting needs.

A number of accounting packages have been developed for microcomputers. Some are fairly simple, while others have features that rival those found on much more expensive minicomputer and mainframe systems. Accounting packages exist for:

- General Ledger
- Accounts Receivable
- Accounts Payable
- Sales Order Entry
- Purchase Order Entry
- Inventory
- Payroll
- Fixed Assets
- Management Analysis

These programs are not designed for highly specialized kinds of businesses nor can they be customized to any great degree, but they frequently offer enough flexibility to meet most small business accounting needs. In a larger corporate setting, the microcomputer may not be used for account processing, but it may be used for quick access to mainframe accounting data and reports. This requires, of course, that the microcomputer is connected to the computer system that handles accounting and that the microcomputer user has authorized access to the accounting database.

7.4 FINANCIAL MANAGEMENT PROGRAMS

A variety of financial planning, forecasting, and management programs is available for microcomputer use. These programs vary widely in their sophistication and complexity, but some have great value for specific applications. They can be used for tracking investments, calculating taxes, and plotting tax strategies. Most fore-casting programs will perform time-series calculations, and some will present results in the form of graphs and charts.

There are also a variety of programs for managing stock portfolios and for tracking particular investments. Several programs designed for personal financial management calculate net worth, manage investments, calculate taxes, estimate insurance and retirement needs, and allow users to set up budgets and balance their checkbooks. A few corporations have been known to purchase and give these packages to selected employees as a special perquisite.

7.5 STATISTICS PROGRAMS

Researchers and others who frequently work with statistics now have the opportunity of using microcomputers for statistical computations. Computers used for calcu-lating statistics have traditionally been "big number" machines capable of handling large volumes of data. Now microcomputer programs provide many of the same programs for statistical processing that were previously only available on mainframe computer systems.

Without the laborious and time-consuming processes of card punching, ver-ification, and often long waits for their research analyses to be batch processed, researchers can directly enter, manipulate, and edit data sets, run analysis, and get their results in a fraction of the time previously required. Statistical programs include analysis of variance, cross-tabulation, multiple regression, and most other modern statistical procedures.

The day-to-day logistics of statistical analysis have long been a burden to researchers. The availability of microcomputer-based statistical analysis tools should prove a time-saving boon to researchers everywhere. Corporations that support such activities should unhesitatingly provide this resource to statistics users when re-quested and expect an increase in research productivity as the result.

7.6 OTHER NUMBER-PROCESSING APPLICATIONS

In addition to already developed and commercially available software for number processing, a great many microcomputer users write their own number-processing programs. The electronic spreadsheet serves as one way users can custom design a needed calculation program, but many such programs have been designed and coded in BASIC language.

Since commercially available programs do not exist for all number processing applications, it may be necessary for users (or other programmers) to develop their own microcomputer programs.

CHAPTER
8

Working with Words

8.1 WORD PROCESSING

In the business world, word processing tends to suffer from a clerical stereotype. While word processing does involve the production of letters and documents, once the exclusive domain of secretaries and typists, it is a far more important concept than just that.

Word processing and the broader concepts of office automation are shaking the foundations of how information should flow within an organization, who should do what tasks, and what is the best way to organize the office for increased efficiency and productivity. Office automation is a new organizational discipline that is having and will continue to have an impact on every corporate employee. Word-processing is at the heart of office automation.

How do microcomputers, word processors, and office automation fit together? It is less than accurate to say that a word-processor system is an electronic typewriter. It certainly can function as one and with great efficiency, but it is far more. It is, at the very least, a much more efficient way of approaching the creation and processing of text-oriented communications.

The contrast between conventional typewriting and word processing needs to be clearly drawn. When the key of a typewriter is pressed and the image of a letter is struck onto the sheet of paper, in essence, four critical functions have taken place. (1) the text has been "entered", (2) the text has been "edited" (i.e., revision will require erasing that character space and restriking, a cumbersome, messy, and often unsatisfactory effort), (3) the text is "formatted" into that single, inflexible spot on the paper, and (4) the text is "printed".

Word processing separates these four functions: *text entry, text editing, text formatting,* and *text printing.* In the word processor, text may be entered and saved in a disk file. At any later time, the *contents* may be edited, altered, revised, added to, or deleted from the original text. At any later time, the format may be altered by changing the line spacing, margins, type style, column width, and a dozen other variables purely for the sake of physical appearance and readability. And, finally, at any later time, the document may be printed, first by a fast-printing, low-quality matrix printer for a rough draft, and then by a slower-printing, letter-quality printer for the final distribution copy.

The significance of the separation of word-processing functions is just beginning to be understood and used productively. Not only does word processing increase the flexibility of physical document production, it also increases the opportunity for revisions, which leads to communications having greater clarity and impact.

Word processing also tends to change *who does what.* An increasing number of business writers and corporate communicators are preferring to enter their text directly into their word processors, forsaking the usual hassle of dictation and messy handwritten drafts.

Some critics argue that word processing actually takes longer than conventional typing. Further studies will answer that criticism. But when it comes to effective business communications, more is at stake than speed. Word choice, readability, correctness, and the total impact of the message must count very heavily in any serious comparison. If it does take longer to prepare a document, it is likely that the extra time is taken up by increased review and editing of the document's contents.

There is reason to believe that, overall, word processing accomplishes more faster, because text entry, text editing, and formatting are all done *on screen* before the final document is printed. Such speed and flexibility make it both practical and economically feasible for any document to go through the necessary number of drafts and/or editing phases.

8.2 WHEN IS WORD PROCESSING APPROPRIATE?

The word-processor approach is appropriate for almost all text preparation tasks, but it is especially appropriate in these cases:

- Whenever a document needs to be done quickly
- Whenever numerous revisions are anticipated

- Whenever several persons will contribute material
- Whenever it consists of standard text
- Whenever a document must be letter perfect
- Whenever one document is used as a pattern for other documents
- Whenever a document is created for different people with only minor but necessary changes
- Whenever a different format or version of the same document is required

Most business letters and documents have these requirements. That may explain why word processing has had almost immediate acceptance in the business world, and it helps explain why word processing is *one of the most frequent microcomputer applications in business* and *the most frequent microcomputer application among nonbusiness users.*

8.3 CAN MICROCOMPUTERS FUNCTION AS WORD PROCESSORS?

A well-equipped microcomputer system can function just as effectively as a dedicated word processor. (Most word processors are, in fact, microcomputers designed exclusively for word processing.) "Well-equipped" means that the microcomputer has appropriate word-processing software, a standard typewriter keyboard, a high-quality video display, and a letter-quality printer.

Should companies buy microcomputers in preference to dedicated word processors? It depends. If a word processor system is to be used exclusively for word processing, then a dedicated system may have special function keys and features that make it easier to use. The movement toward automated offices and *electronic workstations,* however, argues in favor of multiuse, multi-function microcomputers with word processing capabilities, rather than dedicated word processor machines.

8.4 SPECIAL WORD PROCESSING FEATURES

In addition to letter and document production, other text-processing functions and applications fit under the general label of word processing. These include programs that automatically merge different texts, programs that check spelling and grammar, and programs that assist in typesetting.

8.5 DOCUMENT MERGING

Document merging is a word processing function where a standard text is "personalized" for different persons. Because many business communications use the same standard text, letters or documents can be assembled from existing text files.

(Standard or frequently used paragraphs are referred to as "boiler-plate.") A letter or document "template" is created which provides the assembly instructions. The word processor *merges* the text of this letter with each different recipient's name, title, address, salutation, and perhaps some other individual specific information. The appearance of the finished document is that of an individually typed, personal letter. Most word processors, once set into operation, can produce ten, hundreds, even thousands of such letters all automatically with little or no operator attention.

The document merging function is particularly useful for creating legal documents such as contracts which have standard clauses and which must always be letter-perfect. The use of document merging for the creation of legal documents in some law offices has significantly reduced the amount of time and effort traditionally required for this task.

8.6 SPELLING CHECKERS

Programs that check the spelling of words in a given text are available for most microcomputer word processors. These programs read the text file of an existing document and compare the spelling of each word against the program's own internal dictionary. When a mispelling or suspected misspelling is found in the text, it is displayed along with the text in which it appears. The user then has the opportunity to let the program change the spelling or allow the word to stay "as is".

Spelling check programs are highly useful, but their success depends upon the number of words they can verify. If the dictionary handles few words, say less than 30,000, then they are somewhat limited in usefulness. However, most spelling check programs also permit the user to add words which are not in the program list. This feature is especially necessary for organizations that frequently use technical or specialized vocabularies.

8.7 GRAMMAR CHECKERS

A program which works in a fashion similar to the spelling checker will search for punctuation and grammatical errors. Some will also point out stylistic problems such as overuse of the passive voice, and give information on the average length of sentences, readership levels, and so on. While grammar checking programs are limited in what they can do, users can expect to see very sophisticated programs of that type in the future.

8.8 COMPUTERIZED THESAURUS

Still another similar program serves as a thesaurus. When the thesaurus program is run, the user positions the screen cursor over the word for which a synonym is desired and presses a key. The thesaurus program will then display several synonyms for that word. If the cursor is then positioned over one of the synonyms and another key is pressed, the newly selected word replaces the old word in the text. For business writers and communicators who are always looking for that "right word," the computerized thesaurus is a valuable, speedy, and convenient reference tool.

8.9 TYPESETTING

Commercial typesetting is no longer done by hand or by the old standard linotype machines. It is all done electronically and photographically on technically advanced phototypesetting machines. These machines are basically microcomputer word processors coupled with phototypesetting equipment.

Working much like a word-processing typist, the operator enters text into the phototypesetter, and then adds special codes to indicate spacing, leading, type style, and type size. (Type styles and sizes can easily be altered in mid-text with a single command.) Instead of being printed on a printer in the conventional way, the coded information is sent to a phototypesetting camera, which photographically reproduces the text. The result is black and white *camera copy* ready for reproduction.

Microcomputers equipped for communications over a telephone line can send a word-processed text file to a commercial typesetting service to be professionally typeset. If a company needs professional typesetting, this use of the word processor can result in a significant cost savings. Sending a text file to be typeset that has been created and edited by a word processor eliminates the need to reenter all the text into the phototypesetter and much of the redundant proofreading. Since a major cost of typesetting results from paying the typist to enter the text, this word processor-to-phototypesetter approach can save double text-entry costs and can speed up the time required to get typesetting done.

8.10 THE VALUE OF WORD PROCESSING

The value of word processing simply cannot be overstated. With the possible exception of certain tasks, like addressing a single envelope or typing a file-folder label, the word processor outclasses the conventional typewriter everytime. Typists, once they learn to use a word processor, tend to prefer them. Even managers who seldom, if ever, type their own documents (and then perhaps only in the "hunt and peck" tradition) have discovered that the word processor is invaluable for drafting memos, sensitive letters, and a host of other business documents.

Some managers seem to eschew the use of any kind of a keyboard device. Whether it is because they lack keyboard training and skills, or perhaps because they associate the use of a keyboard with clerical-level jobs, they simply do not want anything to do with a device that requires the use of a keyboard. It probably is not to be expected that the word processor will change their minds in this regard.

But if the concern is that "keyboarding" is not a productive use of their time, they ought to give that concern some additional thought.

Managers who give their secretary a memo, letter, or other document to type and then go through a whole series of drafts and re-drafts might well consider the extra time and effort that they would save by simply doing it themselves on a word processor.

A word processor in the hands of a skilled user/manager can be an incredible productivity-enhancing tool. Managers who hesitate to acquire and use a word processor themselves should consider the fact that professional writers (even those who have a near sacred relationship with pen and paper) are switching to word processors in droves. The reason? Productivity. A skilled writer can create and edit drafts much faster, neater, and with greater convenience. But speed is the critical factor. For a professional writer, as for most managers, time is money.

CHAPTER

9

Working
with Graphics

One of the most useful applications of microcomputers in business is their ability
to create graphs, charts, and line drawings. Prior to the introduction of graphics
programs for microcomputers, business graphics were only available on very elaborate and expensive computers, and even when available their use was often limited
to engineering and design applications. The business professional who wanted a
simple pie chart had to draw it freehand or take it to a graphic artist. The process
often took several days even for a single chart. Now microcomputers have opened
up the whole new dimension of computer-generated graphics for business and
professional applications.

9.1 BUSINESS GRAPHICS

The use of graphics in business requires no justification. Business managers have
long used charts and graphs to summarize business data and to communicate business
trends visually. The old saying that "a picture is worth a thousand words" is as
appropriate to business as it is in any other field of endeavor. The pictorial rep-
resentation of numbers as graphs, charts, and drawings often conveys more usable

information than the numbers do by themselves. Microcomputers just make the process of creating those graphics much easier and much faster.

Business graphics are software programs that generate business charts and graphs such as line graphs, scatter graphs, range graphs (high-low-closing), bar charts, and pie charts (see Figure 9.1). Most programs allow the user to construct one or more charts or graphs by entering specifications about the type, size, and labels of the chart and then entering the specific data to be charted. The program then processes this data and displays it on the video display screen.

Some graphics software programs draw charts as either two-dimensional drawings or as three-dimensional perspective drawings. Bars on bar charts can be grouped, or stacked, or grouped in the third dimension. Selected pie-chart slices can be offset from the rest of the pie chart for emphasis. Line charts offer a variety of solid- or dotted-line choices. Area graphs and pie charts offer a variety of crosshatched patterns and colors.

Within limits, these programs allow some creative manipulation. Most programs allow the user to save the data and to construct other charts with different scaling, colors, labels, or placement on the screen. Once the user is satisfied with the image appearing on the microcomputer screen, the finished graph can be printed on a graphics printer or on a special graphics drawing machine called a *plotter*. Graphics produced with a plotter have a very finished, professional look. Using business graphics software, a user can create dozens of presentation-quality graphs in a short period of time. Most plotters allow acetate or Mylar film to be used in place of paper making it possible to create projection transparencies.

9.2 DESIGN GRAPHICS

A second type of graphics supported by microcomputers is *design graphics*. Unlike business graphics, design graphics are intended for making technical drawings and schematics and for drawing models used in the design process. Specific figures can be drawn with different perspectives, rotated into different positions, enlarged, rescaled, and modified by a few keystrokes. Design graphics are used intensively by engineers, draftsmen, and architects for a wide variety of design problems.

A whole new technical discipline has grown up around computer design graphics called computer-aided design or CAD.[1] This specialized area is just starting to be discovered by users outside the engineering and architectural fields, but it is likely that similar programs for microcomputers will be found useful for other business activities. Using these systems, the time required for producing technical drawings is a fraction of that required by hand methods.

Until recently, computer-aided design systems had been programmed only

---

[1]Computer-aided design (CAD) is often coupled with computer-aided manufacturing (CAM). CAD/CAM is a rapidly developing field involving the computer support of design and manufacturing processes.

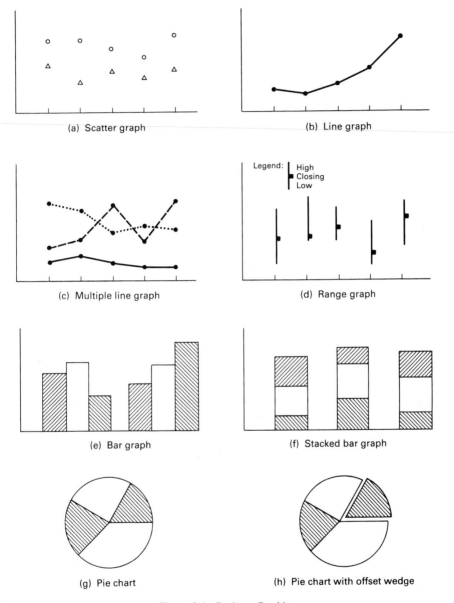

(a) Scatter graph

(b) Line graph

(c) Multiple line graph

(d) Range graph

Legend: High
Closing
Low

(e) Bar graph

(f) Stacked bar graph

(g) Pie chart

(h) Pie chart with offset wedge

Figure 9.1 Business Graphics

for mainframes or minicomputers. Programs are now available that offer similar but somewhat limited capabilities on microcomputers. It should be noted, though, that highly sophisticated CAD systems generally require computers with very large computer memory and processing capabilities—greater than that provided by most microcomputers. Users should not expect microcomputer-based CAD systems to give the same graphics performance that larger systems give unless the microcomputers are specially equipped with components to produce technical graphics.

9.3 ANIMATION GRAPHICS

A third type of graphics available on computers is *animation graphics*. Computer animation is a relatively new field involving the generation of images and whole scenes electronically. Major motion picture films are made using these techniques, but, like CAD, these graphics require very powerful computers. On a somewhat smaller scale, commercial video games make use of computer animation. Their images have quite limited object detail.

Some systems permit mixing video images with computer-generated images. The video or television equivalent of still photographs and motion picture sequences may be stored and retrieved almost *simultaneously* and in any order or sequence. Still pictures can be stored along with textual data in a database. Such systems allow "mug shots" to be included with personnel files or photographs and technical drawings to be cataloged and previewed with all the flexibility and convenience offered by an electronic storage system.

In general, animated computer-generated graphics (not video images) available on a microcomputer are still relatively crude. Typical images use block figures and geometric designs. But the history of microcomputer graphics is a short one, and it is to be expected that new developments in this field will stimulate increased graphics capabilities for business gaming, process illustration, and simulations.

9.4 IMAGE-GENERATING TECHNOLOGY

The creation of computer graphic images requires specialized hardware and software. Not every microcomputer can generate graphics, and the quality of the graphics produced by some is not always acceptable for business applications. A company that plans to use graphics should spend the time and effort to study different graphic systems before investing in what may turn out to be disappointing graphic-generating performance. A number of factors need to be considered both in the selection of microcomputer hardware and software.

9.5 RESOLUTION AND IMAGE QUALITY

The images generated by microcomputers are made up of little dots of light on the video display. Each of these light dots is called a *picture element* or *pixel* or *PEL* (all mean the same thing). Picture elements are arranged on the display screen in rows and columns. The computer controls the picture by turning some picture elements off and others on. The resulting pattern of dots is perceived by the viewer as a line, symbol, or picture.

The quality, sharpness, or degree of picture detail is determined by the number of picture elements that make up a whole picture. The number of picture elements varies from computer to computer. Obviously, the more picture elements that make up the image, the sharper, more detailed the image can be.

The degree of image sharpness and perceptible detail is called a picture's *resolution* and is described in terms of the number of picture elements (pixels) in rows horizontally and by the number of picture elements in columns vertically. Resolutions for microcomputer video displays vary widely. Horizontal resolutions range from 40 to over 1000, with the average near 600. Vertical resolutions range from 16 to over 1000, with the average near 200.

But the numbers alone can be deceiving. The type of phosphors used, the size of the pixel dots, the degree of screen brightness and contrast, the blackness of the background, and, if a color monitor, the saturation of the colors and the method of production all play a role in the quality of the image. Even the size of the screen can make a difference. At a given distance the image on a small video screen tends to look sharper than the same image with the same pixel resolution on a larger screen.

9.6 COLOR OR MONOCHROME?

Microcomputers can produce either full-color displays or monochrome (single-color) displays. Typically, full color displays exhibit from one to four colors simultaneously, although more elaborate systems display 16 colors or as many as 256 colors simultaneously. Monochrome displays produce a single color—white, green, or amber characters on a black background. Most allow characters on the screen to be displayed blinking, highlighted, underlined, or in reversed color (black letters on a white, green, or amber background). These are called *character enhancements*.

Color and monochrome displays typically operate in either *text mode* or *graphics mode*. Text mode is a special mode for displaying high-quality text of very crisp, high-resolution text characters. Graphics mode is used for displaying graphic images. Actually most microcomputers support more than one graphics mode: low, medium, and high resolution. All graphics modes will display text characters, but graphics mode text characters are seldom as legible as text-mode characters. Some monochrome displays will not operate in the graphics mode and are intended only for text applications, however, monochrome displays are generally preferred for word-processing and text-oriented applications.

Color display devices vary considerably in their ability to produce microcomputer displays. Color video displays are of three types: (1) standard color television receivers, (2) composite-signal color monitors, and (3) RGB color monitors.

Standard television receivers produce only very low resolution computer images. They are suitable for some games and very little else. They definitely cannot be recommended for business or professional use. Composite signal color monitors yield sharper images, but they are marginal for prolonged viewing. The RGB (red, green, blue) monitors use separate color electron guns for red, green, and blue primary color images, and they produce a much higher quality image.[2] RGB monitors are the only color display recommended for serious business and professional use.

RGB monitors come in different resolutions, usually advertised as *high-resolution* and *super-high resolution*. All color displays will operate in the graphics mode, but the highest-resolution graphics usually are displayed not in full colors, but in a single color on another colored background.

Color or monochrome? The best answer to this question is "both," but it really depends on the particular application. The best color displays do not usually produce as sharp an image as a high-quality monochrome display (although there are some notable exceptions). If the user is going to spend several hours at a time viewing the display, then a sharp, high-resolution image is a must. Because of its sharpness, a monochrome screen is usually preferred by users for prolonged periods of viewing. Word processing is a typical application where monochrome displays are easier to read and are less tiring over extended periods of use. On the other hand, some programs require color, and the color coding and additional information provided by the colors may be important and necessary.

9.7 SELECTING COLOR AND GRAPHICS HARDWARE

With all the differences in monochrome, color, and graphics displays, how can a user be sure of selecting the right hardware? The decision to purchase microcomputer hardware should be preceded by the opportunity to view, experiment with, and evaluate the image quality firsthand. Evaluations of such equipment should be side-by-side comparisons if possible, using the same programs and displaying identical images.[3]

Microcomputer systems have special circuitry that produces color and/or graphics

---

[2]Red, green, and blue are the electronic primary colors.

[3]Purchasers need to use caution in judging the quality of color displays when viewing the vendor's splashy demonstration programs for purposes of comparison and evaluation. They frequently show only the display's strengths and camouflage any inherent image weaknesses. When evaluating color display capabilities, view a variety of images combining graphics, color, and text—preferably images with which you as a user are already familiar.

images. Some microcomputers allow different circuit boards to be purchased and installed at a later time. The type of color and graphics board used is as critical to the production of quality graphics as is the type of video display used. It is the combination of color/graphics circuit board and video display that determines the type of color and graphics that can be displayed and the quality of images that can be produced.

9.8 HARD-COPY GRAPHICS

Most users of business graphics want a *hard copy* or printed version of the chart. There are two practical ways of doing this. One way is to print the chart using the system's printer *if that printer has a graphics capability.* (Some printers do and some do not.) This method typically produces a black-ink-on-white-paper graph, although there are color graphic printers available. The resolution and detail of such graphics are not equal to that produced by a graphic artist, but for all but a few business uses they are perfectly adequate. A second method is to plot the chart using a graphics plotter. This specially designed piece of equipment actually draws the image using ink pens of various colors. The resolution is very good, and the resulting chart or graph is the next best thing to a graphic artist's rendering. Graphics plotters once cost several thousands of dollars, but now models are priced in about the same range as a printer.

If graphs and charts are used routinely within a company, a microcomputer with a graphics plotter and appropriate software is a good investment and should pay for itself in a short time. A skilled user can generate dozens of c..arts in just a few hours. Also, a graphics plotter is easy to connect and disconnect, making it possible to share a single plotter among other microcomputer users.

9.9 GRAPHIC SOFTWARE

A final word about business programs. When a program is purchased, users should always check to see if it requires color, monochrome, or graphics capabilities. Some programs are designed for graphics and/or color exclusively and will not run at all or will produce unsatisfactory results on monochrome systems.

Users should also note the memory requirements of the programs they plan to purchase. Many color and graphics programs require much more memory than monochrome versions and will not run if the microcomputer system is equipped with too little memory.

Creating and using graphics on a microcomputer is one of the most exciting and potentially important applications of microcomputer technology. While microcomputer graphics are already used for a variety of business tasks, the state of the art steadily advances. All forms of graphics—business, design, and animation graphics—will merge into an extremely powerful microcomputer software system as convenient and easy to use as word processors and spreadsheets.

CHAPTER

10

Data Storage
and Retrieval

10.1 BUSINESS DATA PROBLEMS

Every company has its store of data. Corporate databases containing millions of characters of information detailing every purchase, sale, and transaction are at the heart of most company operations. Service companies deal almost exclusively with data and information. Manufacturers, also, must deal with an increasing glut of data. Handling this kind of high-volume data is certainly not a job for a micro-computer—or a thousand microcomputers. They simply are not designed for that task. It takes a very large computer system to manage great quantities of data day in and day out, year in and year out.

But there are corporate data storage and retrieval problems that are ideally suited to microcomputerization. If one looks for data collections in most companies, one finds, in addition to the very large databases, a host of small collections of data created and maintained both by individuals and departments. File cabinets are obvious places to look, but there are others: the company telephone book, boxes of file cards with customer and sales information, three-ring notebooks of product releases and pricing information, correspondence files, and the inevitable stash of notes and memos that dwell in every manager's desk, to name but a few.

Now obviously all these kinds of data do *not* belong in a computer system.

Simple data collections demand simple methods of storage and retrieval. It may be far easier to flip open a notebook and read a few entries than to call up the appropriate microcomputer program and execute the commands that will retrieve and display wanted information. But if the data to be stored are of a considerable amount (say, over 20 separate items), and if the data need to be retrieved quickly and in different ways, or if the items in the data collection are changing frequently and need to be updated every day or so, then even that data collection may be a good candidate for storage and retrieval on a microcomputer.

The problem with all data storage and retrieval systems is not storage, it is *retrieval*. (It is easy enough to toss those occasional notes and slips of paper into a desk drawer; the problem arises when trying to retrieve one critical note in a hurry.) Ideally, data should be retrievable *flexibly, quickly,* and with a *minimum of effort.*

Flexible retrieval is an especially important concept. In a typical file cabinet system, the chances are good that documents are stored in separate file folders ordered alphabetically or numerically. To retrieve any document systematically, the retriever must know the "key" letters or numbers under which that document was filed (assuming, of course, that the folder is in the file in its logically assigned position.) Regardless of what other identifying information may be contained in the document (such as a date, name, code number, or other specific data), the folder can *only be retrieved* with this one key, the assigned file name or number. This is the problem with all physical file systems. Access is limited to only one access key.

It is possible, of course, through special grouping or color-coding to increase the efficiency of the search by identifying subgroups of folders, but the final retrieval is still dependent on that single key identifier. Electronic (computerized) data storage and retrieval systems provide a better solution.

10.2 ELECTRONIC STORAGE

Electronic storage systems (computer-based data storage and retrieval systems) do not have the limitations that plague physical file systems. The computer stores data as magnetic pulses on tape or disks rather than paper. The storage of data in this way makes it possible to read the data much quicker than is possible with printed words and numbers on paper. The computer can *look at and compare* thousands of items of data in seconds. This process is accomplished so swiftly that it makes it possible to search data records not just by a single key identifier, but by virtually any specific piece of data contained in a file that may be used as a key, or by any combination of different keys. Each separate data item may become a search key if that is necessary. The computer makes it possible to store data efficiently and to retrieve it quickly, efficiently, and flexibly through the use of *multiple keys.*

Take a file of customer information as an example. Suppose the searcher of this data collection wants to retrieve the name of a single individual. If the entries are filed by individual's names alphabetically, retrieval in this case will be straight-forward and easy. But if the entries are filed by company name, retrieval by an individual's name will require looking at every single company entry until the name being searched for is discovered. Even for a modest collection of, say, 1,000 entries, the retrieval process could take hours of painstaking human effort. A computer system, however, could find that entry in seconds.

Take another example. This time suppose that the searcher wants to retrieve a document based on multiple search criteria, say (1) all entries for customers of a certain type, (2) who had done a given volume of business, (3) who had purchased specific products, and (4) who had placed orders since a given date. Again, by hand the task would take hours, perhaps days. Also, since human beings are not especially adept at this sort of task, retrieval errors would be highly likely. For reasons of practicality, such a search would seldom be undertaken.

A computer system can make this multiple-key search, retrieve the desired entries, and print them in a useful form in just seconds. This sort of task is ideal for a computer, and, if the volume of data is not too great, for a microcomputer as well.

Electronic data storage systems offer incredible benefits in terms of retrieval speed, accuracy, and multiple-key search flexibility, but they offer other benefits, too. Such systems require no paper documents, nor do they require a lot of space for storing volumes of paper. They eliminate a great deal of paper handling and "shuffling."

The processes of adding new entries, updating existing entries, or deleting entries are easy and straightforward because it can be done onscreen, just as editing is done during word processing. The results of the update are immediately available for use by all users.

But perhaps the biggest advantage of electronic storage and retrieval systems is that information users can operate these systems by themselves and for them-selves. They can, in most instances, retrieve whatever data they are looking for in less time than it would take to explain to someone else exactly what is to be retrieved.

10.3 THE QUALITY OF BUSINESS INFORMATION

Any information system, electronic or otherwise, should be judged on how well it solves the need for *quality information*. High quality information is information that is *relevant, accurate, well presented,* and available in a *timely* fashion—*in the judgment of the user*. Since *information* is classically defined as *data that have meaning to an individual user*, the assessment of data quality is always an individual judgment call. The distinction between data and information is critical. *Data* are facts. *Information* is data that are meaningful to a particular user. Data become information only as information users find data to be meaningful. A corporate database may contain thousands upon thousands of facts, but these facts do not become information until someone retrieves a few and judges them meaningful and relevant to some corporate decision.

The evaluation of an information system involves asking and answering these four questions:

- Does this system provide the information *I want*?
- Is the information obtained *complete and error free*?
- Is the information presented in a form that *I can readily comprehend and use?*
- Is the information available *when I need it?*

Note that three of these four questions are dependent on what "I" wants. Three of the four factors that govern the quality of information are user dependent. Since only the information user/consumer can make these judgments, it stands to reason that the more the user is involved in data retrieval the greater the probability that the information retrieved will be the information that is really needed.

Microcomputer-based data storage and retrieval systems provide the opportunity for higher-quality information since they are information-user operated. It should, perhaps, be noted that it is the direct involvement of the user that is critical, not the type of system (i.e., microcomputer, minicomputer, or mainframe).[1]

10.4 ORGANIZING DATA FOR STORAGE AND RETRIEVAL

All business microcomputer users who contemplate setting up a microcomputer-based data storage and retrieval system should be aware that business data, as they normally exist, may not be in the best form for storing in a computer data-base system. Storing data without carefully analyzing how the data are structured may forever lock them into particular groupings that defeat some of the benefits provided by electronic storage and retrieval. To take advantage of all the benefits (particularly those involving retrieval flexibility), the data must be reduced to their simplest and most fundamental forms and then organized and structured in ways that ensure that data can be found and retrieved with maximum flexibility. It is not within the scope of this book to discuss how business data can best be structured, but a few data structuring concepts may be useful.[2]

---

[1] A mainframe system operated by the information users would potentially be just as effective.

[2] The analysis of data structures and the creation of database systems is complex. Such analysis is normally undertaken by experienced systems analysts and other highly trained information specialists. If you as a user lack such skills and the database to be created is potentially critical for yourself, your department, or your company, it would be wise to seek consultation or assistance from one of these professionals. No harm will be done to the data themselves, of course, but if your objective is to create a system that will serve your needs for quality information with regard to speed and flexibility of retrieval, professional assistance may be a prudent first step.

10.5 DATA STRUCTURES

For any particular microcomputer application, data are grouped into useful "chunks" to make them easier to store and retrieve. From the smallest to the largest, these chunks of data are *characters, data elements, aggregates, records,* and *files.* (Data elements are also referred to as *data fields.*)

Like a box within a box within a box, files are made up of many records, records are made up of data elements or aggregates of data elements, and data elements are made up of individual characters. Characters, of course, are the smallest unit that can be logically stored.

Data elements are usually the smallest grouping to have a distinctly separate identifying name. Two or more separate data elements that may be used together are called *aggregates.*[3] All the data elements (and aggregates) that are related to one person, object, or entity make up a *record.* Many such records make up a *file.*

This grouping—characters, elements, aggregates, records, and files—is technically called the *data hierarchy* because each larger level is made up of smaller groupings of data (see Figure 10.1).

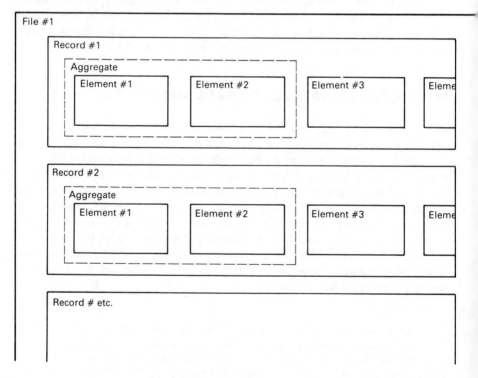

Figure 10.1   Data hierarchy

[3] In a computer system, the *date* consisting of day, month, and year is a typical aggregate, although any one of the three by themselves separately is a data element. Similarly, a *person's name* may be an aggregate consisting of three separate data fields: first name, middle name, and last name.

A tray or rotary file of address cards (Figure 10.2) provides a good example. Each card is a separate record if it contains information about a single individual. Each record contains data elements (or aggregates) consisting of names, addresses, and phone numbers. The total collection of cards makes up the address file.

The term *database* is sometimes used to refer to a collection of files. While this is correct as far as it goes, a true database is more than a collection of files. Technically, databases consist of sets of data specially organized for rapid retrieval using multiple search keys. A true database is developed from an organized and structured set of data elements. These data elements are carefully defined and described in a data dictionary using a standard data description language. Professionally created databases attempt to reduce or eliminate redundancy and make a single repository of data available to different users for a variety of business purposes.

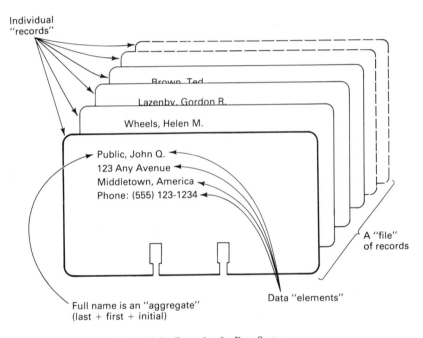

Figure 10.2   Example of a Data System

10.6 COMPUTER FILES

The primary grouping of data in a computer is the *file*. A floppy disk or hard disk contains one or more files. The microcomputer's programs are stored as files, and when a user puts information into a microcomputer and saves it, those data are also stored as a file. Files may consist of application programs, numerical data, or textual data. Any file that the user creates must have a name or identifier. Files logically contain information that is relevant to a particular use. Separate data files may be kept for personnel, inventories, accounting, for spreadsheet activities, word processing text, and thousands of other uses.

Whenever a microcomputer user wishes to retrieve data contained within a particular data file, the disk containing that file must be available in the microcomputer.[4] Usually, data files are stored on a floppy disk (if the file is not too large) or on a hard disk. If the user wants to see what files are on a particular disk, a special program called the *directory* can be executed that will quickly list all the files on a given floppy disk or hard disk.[5]

10.7 DATA RETRIEVAL

When one has an increasing amount of data to keep track of, life can get very complicated in a short period of time. Fortunately microcomputer programs have been written to make life easier. These programs are generically known as *file management programs* or *data management programs*. The more popular term *database* or *database management system* (DBMS) is increasingly used to refer to all types of data handling programs, but a true database program is a very sophisticated data management program that stores and retrieves data in a special way.

In the microcomputer world, two major types of data-management programs currently exist. The simplest are the *computerized filing programs* that allow the user to enter several items of information, then file them electronically. They work with one file at a time and they retrieve whole records. These filing systems go one better than a manual system because information can be retrieved several ways—alphabetically, numerically, or in some other convenient fashion. These programs are useful for very short customer files, catalogs, address or prospect lists, and similar kinds of information collections, but they are severely limited when compared to other, true database management programs. They are generally easy to learn to use and operate. For certain simple data-management tasks, they are unmatchable.

10.8 DATABASE MANAGEMENT PROGRAMS

The second type of data-management program is the true database management systems or DBMS. Database management systems are among the most powerful applications for microcomputers today. These have varying degrees of sophistication and complexity, but are very similar to the data-management programs used in

---

[4]Microcomputers linked to other computer systems also have access to the files of those other systems. A microcomputer is, therefore, not limited just to the files contained on its own disk systems.

[5]Since a hard-disk system may contain hundreds or perhaps thousands of files, the directory does not list all file names at once. Most hard-disk directories group files into hierarchical or tree directories so that only the files for a specific *branch* are listed at one time.

mainframe systems. They often have the same functions and differ only in the amount of data they can store and how fast it can be retrieved within the constraints of a given system. The DBMS allows the user to describe the kind of information that will go into the file, and then for data-entry it will prompt the user when to enter each data item. Data records added to the system can be deleted or edited at any time.

The real advantage of a DBMS is in the retrieval of information. A user types in a request for specific information, and the DBMS program searches, finds, and rapidly displays the information requested. Such requests are called *queries,* and systems that permit this kind of rapid search and retrieval are called *query systems.* Usually the query request is phrased in an English-like form that is easy to learn, remember, and use. The following are typical query-type requests:

SELECT RECORDS FOR LASTNAME = "JONES" AND ACCOUNT > $5,000
SELECT RECORDS FOR BIRTHMONTH = "JULY"

The first query statement tells the system to find and display all the records in the file that include a last name of Jones and where the balance exceeds $5,000.00. The second query command statement tells the system to find and display the records in the file that shows July as the month of birth. Any combination of selection criteria may be used assuming that the data wanted are actually in the system and that the data field name used to recall that particular data item is known.

When data are retrieved from a file, it is a *record* of data that is retrieved. Search keys find records, and, once found, all the information contained on a record is available to be displayed. However, not all the data on any given record needs to be displayed. For example, if out of a file of names and addresses only the names are wanted, then only the name data elements need to be displayed. Most data storage and retrieval systems allow the user to specify not only what records to select, but which data elements from that particular record to display and in what form.

DBMS programs also provide various kinds of *report generation* capabilities. Complete summaries or reports of information can be generated by requesting the DBMS program to find certain information, process it in a specific way, and then format and print the results.

The more sophisticated DBMS programs provide a *procedural command language.* This language makes it possible for the user to save a series of individual commands in a separate command file. The command file can then be executed to do automatically and quickly what each of the commands entered separately would do.

For example, a user might want to retrieve selected data and create a special report. This could be done one command at a time using the query commands. But if the report was one that was wanted frequently or periodically, say once a month or quarterly, these commands could be saved in a procedure file and the report created as needed by simply executing that command-program file.

DBMS software programs are usually offered with special features such as *forms design* for custom designing input and output forms, *math and statistics functions, password protection,* and *data-encryption* (as a measure for improving security of sensitive data). Other features include *text editing, graphics,* and *spreadsheet* capabilities. The trend in microcomputer software development has been to integrate several generic processing programs (including database management systems, spread-sheet programs, and graphics programs) into a single, easier-to-use program. (More will be said about these integrated software programs in Chapter 12.)

Only the more sophisticated DBMS software packages are recommended for business users. While business users may find the simple DBMS programs useful and to their liking, they will be missing many of the advanced capabilities and benefits of microcomputer-based data-management systems. Even though these programs may be a bit more difficult to learn to use initially, the additional effort spent in learning will be more than repaid later. Most users who start with one of the simpler data-management programs will soon see the need to move up to a full-featured DBMS program. Since the advanced DBMS programs will do everything a simpler program will do, it makes sense to start with the more advanced DBMS program from the beginning.

DBMS are among the most powerful and useful software tools available to microcomputer users. Business users who are not able to retrieve data as they want them would do well to consider a microcomputer DBMS as a possible solution.

CHAPTER

11

Data Communications

Data communications refers to data processing that links computer to computer. Although data communications for large computer systems has been around for years, microcomputers have moved into this domain quickly. From a technical standpoint, microcomputers are every bit as capable of data communications as any larger system. While microcomputers are fundamentally stand-alone computers, that is, they do not *require* a connection to any other computer to do useful work, microcomputer users have discovered the value of communicating computer to computer for the purpose of accessing data and program files.

11.1 DATA COMMUNICATIONS APPLICATIONS

There are three common data-communications applications for microcomputers. (see Figure 11.1). Users can:

- Communicate with the *company computer* and its *databases*
- Communicate with *other microcomputers* in a *local area network*

MICROCOMPUTER-TO-MAINFRAME COMPUTER

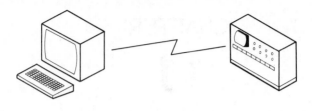

MICROCOMPUTER-TO-MICROCOMPUTER
(local area network)

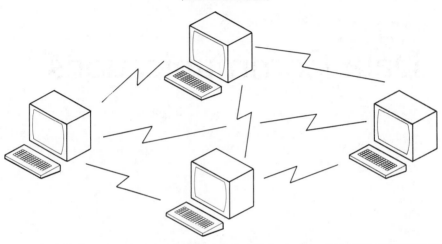

MICROCOMPUTER-TO-REMOTE COMPUTERS
(via dial-up communications)

Commercial
database

Time-sharing
service

User

Other
microcomputers

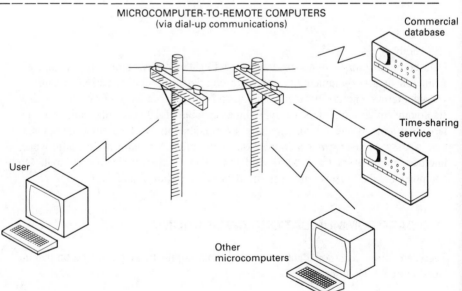

Figure 11.1 Microcomputer Data Communications

- Communicate with *outside computers, time-sharing services, information service databases*

Each of these applications extends the microcomputer user's access to widespread data and information resources.

11.2 ACCESSING THE CORPORATE DATABASE

Independent, stand-alone computing is one of the primary factors leading to the popularity of the microcomputer. But corporate microcomputer users have also been very quick to want to connect their microcomputers to the corporate mainframe computer and its databases.

The major reason for wanting to connect with the company computer is to get data contained in the company database. The company computer system stores data wanted by the microcomputer user, so, rather than obtaining a hard-copy printout and reentering the data into the microcomputer through the keyboard, the user naturally thinks "Why not just connect the two and retrieve data from the data management system of the mainframe computer directly?"

Obviously, it can be done, but doing it is not as simple as saying it. There are both technical and policy problems to overcome.

First, the technical problems. Microcomputers and mainframe computers, while both computers, do not transmit data using the same codes. The microcomputer transmits in a code called ASCII (American Standard Code for Information Interchange) and the mainframe computer transmits in a code called EBCDIC, (Extended Binary Coded Decimal Interchange Code). Before they can understand one another, some translating must be done. The microcomputer's ASCII codes must be translated into EBCDIC, and vice versa.

Also, before the microcomputer and mainframe computer can communicate, they must each send and receive compatible electrical signals. The microcomputer's electrical signals must be converted to those compatible with the mainframe's, and vice versa.

Both problems are easily (if not inexpensively) solved. A special circuit board has been developed that makes the necessary code and electrical signal conversions. This circuit board must be installed inside every microcomputer that is to be connected to the mainframe. An electrical cable completes the connection between the circuit board in the microcomputer and a connection *port* on the mainframe. Every mainframe has a fixed number of ports, so before a microcomputer can be connected, one of these ports must be unused and available.

Once the technical connection is made, a special software program allows the microcomputer user to communicate with the mainframe. The program allows the microcomputer to *emulate* (act like) any other mainframe terminal. In this mode, the program only allows the microcomputer to act like another terminal. It cannot do independent processing while in this mode. But another mode is provided by the program that does allow simultaneous and independent processing. This program allows the microcomputer to *down-load* (retrieve) data from the mainframe to the microcomputer, and to *up-load* (store) data from the microcomputer to the mainframe.

Unfortunately, the problems of microcomputer-to-mainframe data communications do not end there. Certain other issues must be resolved as well.

Some mainframe data-processing managers may be very reluctant to allow microcomputer users to access the mainframe systems using microcomputers, especially if the connection can be made by an outside telephone line. Such a connection increases the opportunity for unauthorized access to the corporate computer and its databases. The security and integrity of the corporate data are at increased risk.

When a microcomputer emulates a computer terminal, the risk is no greater than it would be with another terminal. Terminal emulation, therefore, presents no particular hazard because all the security provisions in effect for other terminals are also in effect for the terminal-emulating microcomputer. Likewise, when the microcomputer is merely down-loading data to be used by the microcomputer for an independent application, there is very little risk.

A potential, but very real, problem arises when the microcomputer is capable of up-loading data to the corporate database. Mainframe computer programs are designed to ensure that all data going into the database are "pure." These programs check and recheck for accuracy. Even a small error can be very costly for a company. Data accuracy is critical.

The process of up-loading files from a microcomputer to a mainframe does not necessarily utilize the mainframe software that checks data as they are entered. The microcomputer user, intentionally or unintentionally, can escape these necessary safeguards. While the user may simply want to use the data-storage facilities of the mainframe and may have only the purest motives, the opportunity to up-load increases the vulnerability of the system and increases the risk of contaminating corporate data.

In general, mainframe data-processing managers would prefer not to give "outsiders" any opportunity to contaminate their "pure" data. Some managers have been known to get outright hostile at the mere mention of connecting a microcomputer to the corporate mainframe. With the responsibility for maintaining the integrity of the corporate databases weighing heavily on their shoulders, who could blame them?

But access to the corporate databases through the use of microcomputers is rapidly becoming a fact of corporate life. If the need to access the corporate data base is sufficiently legitimate, most managers are willing to work out a compromise. One typical compromise is to permit data to be down-loaded to the microcomputer but to not permit data to be up-loaded to the mainframe.

Yet another reason for wanting to connect a microcomputer to the corporate mainframe computer is simply for the purpose of using the mainframe computer. Users who must work with both microcomputers and the company mainframe system find it more convenient to have one all-purpose microcomputer/terminal on their desk rather than two. Since the emulated terminal is subject to the same password provisions and mainframe software, the data security and data integrity are not an issue.

11.3 NETWORKING

Microcomputers can also be connected with other microcomputers. Microcomputers connected in this way are said to be *networked*. The connection generally requires that each microcomputer be equipped with a special circuit board and connecting cables. Theoretically, from two to several hundred may be connected in this fashion, but in practice, a microcomputer network will consist of less than 100, and very probably will consist of 4 to 30 microcomputers in one single network. If the microcomputers are all located in close proximity (say, in the same building) but are not connected through telephones or an existing mainframe system, they are said to be part of a *local area network* (LAN). This term is used to distinguish between local, microcomputer-only networks and larger networks that include several mainframe or minicomputers and their associated terminals. If microcomputers are linked to participating mainframe systems, then they, of course, participate in the larger network.

Users in a LAN can share hard-disk storage, printers, plotters, and other *peripherals*. The savings realized by not having to purchase duplicate printers and other equipment is obvious (assuming that the cost of the network is less than the cost of additional hardware). The major advantage of a LAN, however, is that several users can access the same data files.

11.4 ELECTRONIC MAIL

Electronic mail is the ability to send memos, letters, and documents electronically. Most electronic mail systems utilize computer networks for storing, retrieving, transmitting, and managing such mail, and most mainframe systems generally have, at a minimum, some sort of message-exchange system available to users. Microcomputer users can also participate in electronic mail systems, including those principally serving mainframe computer users.

There are several types of electronic mail systems, all dependent on the kind of interconnections between senders and receivers. The first type is called a *closed system*. In a closed system, both the senders and the receivers work with the terminal or microcomputer directly. The closed system requires each user to have a microcomputer or a mainframe terminal and to be connected into a network. This network may consist exclusively of mainframe users, exclusively of microcomputer users (operating in a local area network), or a mixture of the two. Many companies already have mainframe data-communication networks (telecommunications) that link users in distant cities into the same network. In a network, it is a relatively simple matter to set up electronic addresses and to train users in the use of the electronic mail system.

Open-system electronic mail systems are of two kinds. The first is similar to the closed system, where the message originator sends the message by computer and the recipient also receives the message by computer. It differs from the closed system in that the message is electronically handled by an intermediate carrier service such as The Source's *SourceMail* service, CompuServe's *EMAIL* service, GTE-Telenet's *Telemail* service, Western Union's *EasyLink* service, and others. Both the message sender and the message receiver must subscribe to the service.

The second type of open system only requires that the sender have access to a computer and subscribe to the service. The message is delivered to the recipient as paper mail. The sender originates the message by a computer linked to a local electronic mail service. The electronic mail service then electronically forwards the message to a station near the recipient. That station then makes a paper copy of the message, puts it into an envelope, and delivers it to the recipient either through the U.S. mail or by private courier.

In open systems the message sender is billed for the service. However, to receive mail electronically from The Source or CompuServe, the recipient must also subscribe to that service. The recipient is not charged directly for the mail but must pay the usual hourly rate for whatever time the user is connected to the service.

The U.S Postal Service offers an electronic mail service called E-COM. The final message is printed, placed in a blue envelope, and delivered by conventional mail delivery. Currently, the users of this service must send E-COM messages in quantities of at least 200.

Western Union gives users access to the same service on a single-letter basis. They collect E-COM messages until they have a group of 200 and then forward them on to the U.S. Postal Service for delivery. MCI offers a similar service, MCI-MAIL, worldwide. It is also possible to access Western Union's TELEX network for similar services. The charges for these services range from less than $1 to more than $25 per message for overnight or guaranteed four-hour delivery.

Microcomputer systems can be set up for automatic electronic mail transfer at night or during hours the systems are not otherwise in use. These systems are called *unattended data-communications* and operate as follows. A microcomputer is programmed (easily done with commercially available software) to automatically dial up another microcomputer in the receiver's city. Once the two microcomputers have established contact, any messages waiting in the system are sent to the receiving microcomputer system over the phone line. Each message is sent as a separate message file. After the message transfer, the systems automatically disconnect. Messages are then distributed to each respective addressee. In such systems, all stations must be equipped with the same microcomputer programs and, of course, be equipped for data communications.

How does electronic mail work for the user? Basically, all electronic mail systems work the same way. The message originator logs-on to the electronic mail service or network program, enters the recipient's address (name, service account number, or special code), types the message, and presses a single key to speed it along its way. At the receiving end, users log on to the same electronic mail service or network program and press a single key to see if new messages have arrived since the last log-on. The messages can then be read, erased, saved in a computer file, or printed out.

Some electronic mail systems have useful features like the ability to send a long document, to automatically send a message to a group of predefined recipients, to send blind copies, to forward mail to other electronic addresses, to assign priorities (so an urgent message is seen first), and to request return receipts ensuring that the message was received. Some systems also have provisions for encrypting messages to ensure privacy and confidentiality.

Who needs electronic mail? The presumed primary benefit of electronic mail is speed. Theoretically, a message can be sent and received (even using the paper mail delivery method) in much less time than conventional mail. So far, most electronic mail systems have not proved themselves to be significantly faster, more convenient, nor more economical than conventional mail services for the bulk of most business mail. There are a few exceptions, of course, and these systems improve daily. If the message absolutely must be received in the shortest possible time, there is probably no better alternative than electronic mail.

If a company already has a data-communications network in place and there is a high volume of paper mail that flows from persons and locations served by that network, electronic mail may not only speed up the delivery but may significantly reduce mail costs.

While it has been predicted that electronic mail systems will eventually replace paper mail systems, that does not seem to be happening very fast, probably because most corporate users do not have access to a terminal or a microcomputer. Put another way: most corporate employees do not yet have an "electronic address." It does seem likely, however, that, as mail volumes increase, as delivery times become increasingly critical, as private data-communications networks expand, and as electronic carrier service rates decrease through competition, electronic mail will become a primary mode of delivery for business mail.

11.5 DIAL-UP DATABASES

In addition to the exchange of information that originates inside the company, microcomputers are capable of accessing a wealth of information that is available outside the company. Such external information is often useful for economic and strategic business planning. Services known as *dial-up databases* are a source of such information.

Dial-up databases are essentially computer-based libraries and repositories of business, scientific, technical, and general information. There are more than 500 such databases worldwide that can be accessed through data communications. With a microcomputer system equipped for data communications, access is easy. The user contacts the database sponsor by phone or mail and arranges to become a subscriber. The user is given a dial-up telephone number to access the system, an account number, and a password. To log-on to the service, the user simply dials the database access number and then enters the password and account number as requested. The database service will respond with a message welcoming the user to the service and will display a menu of activities from which the user can select. After completing whatever activities have been chosen, the user logs off by selecting the "quit" option.

What kind of information can be accessed from a dial-up database? The variety is extensive, but the emphasis is generally on current information. Database sponsors go to great lengths and expense to keep information up to date. Currency of information is one of the important benefits of these services. The topics of information range from the trivial to the most complex technical data. From some databases, a user would get factual reports and data. From others, the user would get only references to other documents. Researchers, in particular, are often interested in research studies done by others. They can use the database repository to look through hundreds or thousands of research studies to find just those of particular interest.

Typically, the user will specify a set of key words and will request the system to retrieve only those references with the key words in the title. The system then responds with bibliographic listings of titles, author's names, sources of the full document, and an abstract or summary of the article's contents. In one or two hours, a user can accomplish work that might take a researcher days or months to do by hand.

Database service companies that provide microcomputer access include Lockheed Corporation's DIALOG system containing more than 170 databases on scientific and technical information, Systems Development Corporation's ORBIT system with more than 68 databases, Bibliographic Retrieval Service's STAIRS with more than 30 databases, and the National Library of Medicine's MEDLINE system with more than 17 databases on health delivery and administration.

Other databases of particular business interest include The Source, CompuServe, and Dow Jones News/Retrieval. Information available from these dial-up systems includes general news, weather, sports, business news from the *Wall Street Journal, Barron's,* and the Dow Jones News Service, text search of past news stories, corporate financial information, earnings forecasts, current and historical Dow Jones quotes, and economic information. These on-line information services even provide access to the OAG/EE (Official Airline Guide/Electronic Edition) for information on flights and fares, and access to electronic shopping and banking services. Attorneys and others interested in the law can access West Law's legal data base for federal and state statutes and cases.

The use of dial-up database services, while not widely known by the general public, is definitely on the increase. In the five years between 1974 and 1979, the number of searches conducted rose from 700,000 to over 4,000,000. This was before microcomputers came into general use. Now that they have, they will undoubtedly stimulate even greater use of dial-up databases. A rapid growth in this industry is expected.

11.6 COMBINED VOICE/DATA COMMUNICATIONS

Technical developments in telephone communications have made it possible to transmit both regular telephone voice conversations (voice communications) and computer data (data communications) over the same telephone line. Simultaneous voice/data communications decrease the overall cost of separate systems and simplify the communication process.

These systems provide users with the convenience of rapid retrieval phone number directories, automatic dialing, redialing until answered, unattended electronic mail transfers, voice and message store and forwarding, time and date stamping of messages, conference calling, simultaneous voice/data/graphics communications, slow-scan video image transmission, and a host of other features that promise greater communications efficiency and personal productivity.

11.7 DATA COMMUNICATIONS HARDWARE

Communication with other microcomputers requires special devices that may or may not be part of the original hardware purchase. The equipment required depends on the type of communications link. Connecting microcomputers to a mainframe computer requires one type of circuitry. Connecting microcomputers together in a local area network requires yet another type of circuitry. Setting up a microcomputer to communicate through the telephone lines requires still another type of circuitry. In every case, equipping a microcomputer for data communications is a matter of purchasing and installing the appropriate circuit boards and software.

The most common form of microcomputer data communications is via the telephone. A telephone link makes use of a device called a *modem*. (Modem is an abbreviated way of saying *mod*ulator/*dem*odulator.) The modem sends data by first converting (modulating) the digital bits of the microcomputer into an audible analog signal that can be transmitted on a standard telephone line. Since data are also received by the microcomputer, the modem also reverses the process and converts (demodulates) incoming analog signals back into digital signals. Modems have other features, but the conversion process is their stock in trade.

Modems are available as separate pieces of equipment, or they are available as circuit boards that are installed inside the microcomputer's cabinet. Older modems, called *acoustical* modems, require that the telephone handset be placed in "cups" on the modem. Newer modems allow the telephone line to be plugged directly into the modem itself.

Modems for microcomputers come in a variety of transmitting and receiving speeds. A low speed modem transmits and receives at a maximum of 300 bps (bits per second), which is about 30 characters per second. A medium speed modem is rated at 1200 bps which is about 120 characters per second, and a high-speed modem is rated at 2400 bps or 240 characters per second. All modems transmit and receive in a similar fashion. The only difference is that one transmits and receives at a rate that is slower or faster.

For home use or infrequent business use, a 300-bps modem is generally adequate. For frequent business use, the 1200- or 2400-bps modems save a considerable amount of user time and are likely to be more cost efficient. At current prices, the higher-speed modem costs a little more than twice as much as a low-speed modem.

Another device, called a *serial interface* is a circuit board that is required for data communications (and for some types of printers). The computer internally transmits several (usually 8 or 16) bits simultaneously along parallel circuits. A two-conductor telephone line cannot easily handle more than one bit at a time, so a device is needed to *serialize* the data bits, that is, to string them out one after the other like beads on a string. This is the job of the serial interface circuit. Some microcomputers come equipped with a serial interface. Others require the purchase and installation of this special circuit board as an option.

11.8 DATA COMMUNICATIONS SOFTWARE

Just as microcomputers need special hardware to communicate, they also need a special communications program. The communications program controls and coordinates the two-way exchange of data being sent from the computer, as well as that being received by the computer. Since the binary bits are sent serially (remember the beads on a string analogy), the receiving microcomputer must know when a group of bits starts and when it stops, how many bits are being sent, and other information.

There are different methods for grouping and sending these signals. Particular groupings are called *communications protocols*. Most protocols specify the number of data bits sent for each character (usually seven or eight), the number of *stop-bits,* and if parity checking is used, whether it is *odd* or *even*.[1] Two microcomputers engaged in two-way data communications must have software with matching communications protocols; otherwise, the data sent cannot be properly interpreted by the receiving microcomputer and the data appear garbled.

Both the sending and receiving microcomputers must be equipped with a data-communications software program, and both programs must be set to the same protocol. The data-communications software program allows the user to set and change protocols as necessary to communicate with different computer systems.

---

[1]Parity is a method used to check for transmission accuracy. After transmission, the 1 bits for each byte (group of 7 or 8 bits) are totaled to determine if they are *odd* or *even*. A missing bit will cause failure of the parity check and that byte will be retransmitted. Communications protocols can be set to check for either odd or even parity.

In addition to setting protocols, most data-communications programs have features that allow setting up a directory of telephone numbers, automatic dialing, repeat dialing, automatic log on to other computer systems and database services, automatic answering (for unattended operation), sending and receiving of data files, saving received files to disk, and changing how information appears on the screen. These special-feature programs automatically relieve the user from having to fuss with various technical operations.

Without data-communications capabilities, a microcomputer is still a powerful, independent data-processing device. However, with data-communications capabilities, the microcomputer user gains almost unlimited information and data-processing opportunities. Access to corporate database information, access to outside databases, exchange of information along networks and with other users, and access to mainframe data-processing power—all these windows of data and information access are thrown open to the user at the touch of a few keys.

12

Other Business Applications

Up to this point, the discussion of microcomputer applications has centered on the generic processes—*number processing, word processing, graphics processing, data storage and retrieval,* and *data communications.* While this five-part classification of applications makes the whole range of microcomputer applications easier to understand, real-world computing is not so obligingly divided. Day-to-day business microcomputing is problem oriented. Users use their microcomputers to help solve business problems, and the activities involved in solving business problems typically include working with a mix of data-processing types all at the same time. A particular problem may be fundamentally a number problem, but the solving of that problem may involve working with words, graphics, and data storage and retrieval.

12.1 INTEGRATED APPLICATIONS SOFTWARE

Although early microcomputer software was developed to deal with single, generic processes, it soon became clear that combining generic functions into the same program would make microcomputing more convenient and users more productive. With single-purpose generic software, a user working with a spreadsheet program needing to retrieve data from a data-management program would have to stop work on the spreadsheet, exit that program, load the data-management program, give whatever commands were necessary to retrieve the needed data, copy the data on a scrap of paper so it would not be forgotten, exit from the data-management program, reload the spreadsheet program, and finally enter the retrieved data into the spreadsheet. With integrated software programs, that same task could be done with much less trouble. From the spreadsheet the user would press a couple of keys to enter the data-management portion of the program, retrieve the data, and press a couple of more keys to return to the spreadsheet. Users no longer had to stop one operation to begin another.

Integrated software programs combine various generic programs like spreadsheets, word processors, graphics generators, database management systems, and data-communications programs into one integrated program. The user can move from one program function to another with relative ease.

There are numerous benefits to integrated software, but an important one has been that the user has to learn only one set of commands. Because generic programs were developed independently and by different software developers, they each had their own particular set of commands. Each new program meant that the user had to learn yet another operating language. To complicate the matter, authors of these programs used different words to command the same program activity, or the same words to command a quite different program activity. This mixture of commands is always confusing to the user, and switching from one generic program to another was an exercise in frustration. Fortunately, integrated software programs have done much to ameliorate this source of user frustration.

Integrated software programs have solved yet another problem for users of generic software. That problem is data-file compatibility. Single-purpose generic programs do not necessarily store data in the same data formats. This often makes it impossible for users to use the same data files in two different programs. For instance, a user might create a spreadsheet solution using a generic spreadsheet program, but wish to include the spreadsheet results in a report created using a generic word-processing program. If the data-file types are not compatible, it cannot be done without first figuring out a method of translating the data to a compatible format.

Integrated software solves the problem of data format compatibility by using the same data storage format for all functions. Some integrated programs even go so far as to allow the user to specify the data format desired so that data files generated using the integrated software can be used with any other applications program.

The integration of software has been received so enthusiastically by microcomputer users that many commercial software developers are now focusing much of their product development efforts on integrating more and more functions. It is likely that most commercial software developers will continue to develop programs that offer increasing integration of many diverse data-processing functions.

A special group of microcomputer programs recently introduced to the marketplace addresses the problem of getting single-purpose generic programs to work together in a more integrated way. Many users have grown attached to their old, familiar software and are reluctant to throw it all away and purchase a new integrated package. The *integrator* programs provide a solution.

These programs, in effect, provide an umbrella or "shell" program under which generic programs can be active or in use more or less at the same time. The program provides a menu that allows any resident program to become the active or *foreground* program. Each application can be "popped up" on the screen as a separate "window." Users have the same quick access to different applications as they would using a true integrated package. Data incompatibility may still remain a problem although some integrators provide a utility program that can be used to convert data files from one format to another.

The real advantages to these programs are that they permit the user to include virtually any program within their own customized integrated software system (including other integrated software programs), and they permit the user to continue using generic software that they know and like.

12.1 DESK UTILITIES

While the use of microcomputers undoubtedly adds a measure of complexity to our lives, some programs are destined to make business life easier. One group of such programs is the desk utilities. These programs replace with their microcomputerized equivalent such necessary functions as:

- Calendars
- Clocks
- Appointment schedules
- Note pads
- Message and memo pads
- Telephone directories
- Address files
- Programs that will reorganize a list of items alphabetically
- Programs that will dial the phone
- Programs that will make the microcomputer and printer act just like a typewriter (useful for typing envelopes, file-folder labels, and quick notes)
- Programs that provide templates of commonly needed business letters
- Programs that turn the microcomputer into a ten-key, multifunction calculator
- Programs that store formulas and allow the user to quickly solve business equations just by entering the appropriate values
- Programs that let the user generate a list of things to do
- Programs that allow the user to set an alarm clock or alarm calendar that gently presents a reminder of an appointment or a task that may need attention some days in the future

There are even desk utilities that let the user record expense account information and then provide daily, weekly, and monthly summaries. Unfortunately, they have not programmed a microcomputer to bring a cup of coffee—at least not yet.

12.3 STRICTLY FOR PROGRAMMERS

There are other utilities of interest to users who write their own microcomputer programs. These programs help programmers plot flowcharts and design program logic, help generate code, edit program text, design screen layouts, make special listings of code, determine inefficient sequences of code so the execution time can be improved, produce cross references of program variables, write program documentation, and provide a virtual "toolbox" of useful program development tools.

12.4 PROJECT MANAGEMENT

Project management is yet another area in which microcomputers are proving to be most useful. Those who manage major projects involving numerous job tasks and extensive resources and extending over several weeks or months are finding a microcomputer coupled with appropriate project management software to be an exceptionally useful management tool.

Most large projects require the project manager to identify project tasks, task durations, task dependencies (i.e., one task cannot begin until an earlier task has been completed), task resources, and project costs. All these factors must be planned and anticipated in advance of the actual project initiation. But they also frequently change during the course of a project, and each change may affect the date of task completion and the level of resource consumption. It is necessary for the project manager to stay on top of these changes and take actions to keep the project on track and to bring the project in on time and within budget.

Without help in monitoring these changes and their impact, a manager is soon lost in the complexity and detail of shifting schedules and uncontrolled costs. The "big picture" in large projects, once lost, is very difficult to recapture.

A computerized project-management program helps the project manager track all these changes and generates documents that keep the project manager informed about a project's status. Typically, these programs will produce Gantt charts for tracking activity start dates, stop dates, and task dependencies; critical-path networks for ensuring that project activities will not be delayed due to unavailable resources; and project cost reports for planning, budgeting, resource allocation, and consumption monitoring. Computerized project-management systems allow changes to be made at any moment, and they create reports that are current with the last data entered. Also, the documentation of project activities is usually of better quality than is usually the case with project-management systems where updates are done infrequently, if at all.

The control that is possible with a computerized system greatly exceeds that of a manual system. Such systems will not make a good project manager out of a poor one, but they will make a good project manager a more efficient one.

12.5 COMPUTER-BASED INSTRUCTION

Another exciting application of microcomputers is for increased education and training. Although computerized instruction has been supported on mainframe systems for quite a number of years, the microcomputer is stimulating the increased use of computer-based corporate training. Computers have long been known for their value as teaching machines, but until low-priced microcomputers appeared on the scene, computerized instruction was prohibitively expensive for most companies. Microcomputers now make computer instruction not only possible, but a highly important resource for all types of corporate training, including training in the use of microcomputers themselves.

Microcomputers make ideal tutors because they can be programmed to work interactively with users. A well-designed computer-based training (CBT)[1] program presents information (using text, graphics, and animation), solicits a response to questions and problems, evaluates the response, and then feeds information back to the student on the correctness of the response.

Computerized instructional programs can adapt to the needs of different students by presenting additional drill on areas of knowledge that are weak or by skipping over sections of material in which the student is already knowledgeable. The microcomputer can exactly match the student's learning rate, moving ahead only as the student moves ahead or waiting patiently for the student to respond.

In head-to-head competition with other forms of instruction, computerized instruction has held its own. It even has a slight edge in cost effectiveness. The microcomputer provides not only an effective way to present instruction, but, in the areas where it is appropriate, it also provides a more economical way for instruction to take place.

Microcomputers have several significant advantages over other instructional approaches. They can be placed anywhere, they require no special classroom, and, once set up, they keep delivering the same, consistent-quality instruction to student after student with almost no increase in cost.

Of course computer-assisted instruction can only be as good as the *courseware* (i.e., instructional software) that is used. Poorly designed instructional programs

---

[1]Computerized instruction travels under several aliases including computer-based instruction (CBI), computer-assisted instruction (CAI), computer-based education (CBE), and computer-based training (CBT). All terms basically refer to the same thing, that is, instruction delivered through the medium of the computer. Another related term is computer-managed instruction (CMI) which generally refers to the use of a computer for the purpose of giving tests and tracking test scores and student achievement.

will be ineffective regardless of how they are used or who they are used with. Although there is not presently a great deal of courseware available, more is being introduced all the time.

A chief disadvantage of most commercially produced courseware programs is that they are designed to deal with the needs of a general audience and often do not address the specific training needs of any given company or department. Highly relevant courseware may be difficult to come by for corporate training unless the courseware is produced in-house.

This can be done with course-development "authoring" software, which converts instructional information into a microcomputer instructional presentation. But coding instruction to be presented by computer has never been a big problem. The difficulty lies in the design of instructional activities in the first place. This can only be done effectively by those with specialized instructional design knowledge and skills. Despite the current paucity of good training courseware, microcomputers will likely become a major mode of corporate training.

12.6 THINKER TOOLS

It is appropriate to end this section on microcomputer applications by reflecting on two different types of software that affect our thinking and information processing in very different ways. The first type might be called *convergent process* programs and the second type, by contrast, might be called *divergent process* programs. The first type, convergent, allows the user to converge on a specific solution or outcome. Programs of this type are based on the idea that (1) certain data are input, (2) the data are acted on by very specifically defined processes, and (3) a predefined or very predictable result is output. This type of software accounts for almost all software created and in use for both microcomputers and mainframe computers.

The second general type of software, divergent, works similarly, but the outcome is different. Programs proceed in this fashion: (1) certain data are input by the user, but the program also adds input or modifies the data input by the user, (2) the user specifies particular processes, but these processes can have random or highly complex and conditional effects, and (3) the output is somewhat unpredictable. Rather than the outcome *converging* to a *specific* result, the outcome *diverges* into a *unique* result. Something new has been created.

In divergent processing, the interaction between the user and the computer program is apt to be highly *iterative*. That is, the user proceeds through many "cycles of approximation" until satisfied with the successively changing outcome. The very act of computing itself changes the nature of what is input and output almost continuously. The final result is not wholly predictable, but then neither is it disappointing.

A microcomputer equipped with this second type of software becomes an instrument of creativity. It has a synergetic effect that expands and extends the thinking modes and capacity of the user. A descriptive name for programs of this second type might be *thinker tools,* because they are tools for stimulating a high degree of cognitive and creative activity.

Divergent programs are those that allow the user to *construct* an answer. The programming language LOGO is a good example. So are the graphics programs that allow the user to construct drawings from primitive geometric forms, or to rotate, explode, or distort figures in a progressive series of design elaborations.

An electronic spreadsheet also functions frequently as a thinker tool. Even though the user's purpose may be to construct a spreadsheet model that will function ultimately as a convergent program (where specific data are input, processed in a specific way, and a predictable result is output), the act of creating a spreadsheet takes place in a divergent fashion.

The process of building a spreadsheet is, in and of itself, creative. As formulas and data values are entered and the results studied, the user begins to see new possible relationships and experiments with new formulas and data values. The resulting model may become quite complex and bear little similarity to the spreadsheet model originally envisioned. Usually it is better. The thinking processes engaged in by the user have been stimulated. The product is not a fulfillment of the program, but a new creation. *Voilà!*

A new class of microcomputer programs called *thought processors* or *idea processors* are directed at this kind of divergent data and information processing. These specialized software programs are designed to help the user carry out the creative mental processes and tasks that every writer engages in to some degree whether composing a memo, letter, report, proposal, article, book, or, for that matter, any type of text-oriented document.

Help is provided in three ways: (1) by making it possible to capture and organize ideas flexibly, (2) by assisting with the "housekeeping" chores of writing, and (3) by providing document templates and models.

The creation of a document of any significant length involves brainstorming for new ideas, researching, note taking, filing, making annotations, labeling, sorting, creating lists and outlines, and generating drafts. Thought processors make it easy to quickly generate lists of ideas and to sort, label, and prioritize these ideas for future reference.

They also make it easy to organize ideas into an outline form consisting of any level of subordination and detail. The outlines can then be expanded with full text or moved to any other level in the outline at will. Links can be established to connect any idea structure (blocks of words, sentences, paragraphs, or whole sections of text) with any other. The screen-oriented nature of the thought processor allows the user to capture and experiment with ideas flexibly. Freezing ideas too early in the formative stages of writing tends to block insight and creativity.

Idea processors also provide models and templates that can be quite useful. The standard form for a business letter is an often used template, and many companies have dozens of standard or model letters that simplify the letter writer's job. Other templates and models that may be provided by an idea processor are those for policy statements, job descriptions, planning documents, end-of-year reports, staff evaluations, sales proposals, contracts, client records, résumés, product descriptions, systems analyst's reports, cost-benefit studies, and more.

The thought processors and other divergent-type programs are just beginning to come into their own. Their contribution will not be to replace human creativity, but to extend it in, as yet, unforeseen ways. The use of the microcomputer as a tool for thinkers is just beginning.

CHAPTER

13

A Corporate Decision: To Microcompute or Not to Microcompute

Microcomputers are currently in use in hundreds of large corporations and thousands of smaller businesses. This fact alone may be enough to convince other companies to purchase and use them. But while there are many legitimate reasons for using microcomputers, there are also some valid arguments against using them.

Should every company use microcomputers? Perhaps. Perhaps not. The microcomputer is becoming an extremely valuable tool, and it is likely that most companies will find the microcomputer useful and appropriate for at least some information-processing tasks. But every company *should* at least study the microcomputer issue and decide for itself.

13.1 REASONS FOR NOT USING MICROCOMPUTER TECHNOLOGY

There are some very salient reasons why a company might decide not to use microcomputers, or might decide to defer their use until a later time. Some of these reasons are as follows:

1. The applications intended for computerization are too complex and difficult to be handled by microcomputers.

2. The task to which microcomputers will be applied is not automated, and the company is not yet ready to suffer the agonies of conversion.
3. The company already has resources and technology that will do the job.
4. Plans have been made for end-user computer use and such plans do not include microcomputers.
5. The company acknowledges the potential of microcomputers but does not wish to incur the additional costs necessary for training and support services.
6. The company is concerned that, with the current rapid changes in computer technology, any systems acquired now would quickly become obsolete; they would prefer to wait for new developments

Each of these reasons is considered in more detail.

Applications Intended for Computerization are Too Complex and Difficult to Be Handled by Microcomputers

This is indeed a legitimate reason for not adopting microcomputer technology. It is a fortunate company that finds it out before making the investment. Small companies, especially those with no previous experience using computers and automated systems, are most prone to make this mistake. Presumably they feel they can "ease into computers" by starting first with a microcomputer system; but if they attempt using the system for high-volume transactions, complicated accounting, or extensive inventory control, they may soon discover that microcomputer systems just do not have the capacity and power to do what needs to be done.

The Application Task to Which Microcomputers Will Be Applied Is Not Automated, and the Company Is Not Yet Ready to Suffer the Conversion Process

If a business operation needs to be automated, putting it off will not ease the situation. But the process of automating is never simple. Hardware and software alone do not make an automated system. Company policies and procedures often need to be thought through and rewritten, and personnel need to be retrained.

Also, the changes wrought by automation may involve stresses that challenge a company financially and managerially. This too is a legitimate reason for not adopting microcomputers, at least until the challenge is ready to be met.

The Company Already Has Resources and Technology That Will Do the Job

Strange as it may seem, more than a few companies have purchased microcomputers to do a job where there was already mainframe or minicomputer hardware and software available. There are several reasons why this happens.

One is the classic case of the left hand not knowing what the right hand is doing. An individual or department simply purchases a microcomputer system without asking someone in the know if such a computer capability already exists.

Another possibility is that the user simply wants to "do it on a micro," and no one questions or is bothered by the duplication of resources.

Yet another possibility is that the relationship between the microcomputer user and the corporate data-processing department is not a particularly friendly relationship. It may simply be "politics."

Sometimes companies are justified in using microcomputers in spite of the fact that other resources are available. On the other hand, electing not to use microcomputers because other equally effective computer resources exist is a very good reason.

Plans Have Already Been Made For End-user Computer Use and Such Plans Do Not Include Microcomputers

This can be a legitimate reason, but the reason itself needs to be fully understood. Some data-processing organizations take the broadest possible view of both the company's data-processing needs and of individual information-user's needs. They conscientiously plan for comprehensive user networks and take great effort to provide adequate end-user systems. These well-engineered end-user systems are usually superior to unplanned or incompatible microcomputer-based systems that cannot communicate with each other. In this event, the reason for not using microcomputers seems fully justified.

However, some data-processing departments are simply fearful of giving up their exclusive control of information and data-processing resources, microcomputers included. They therefore promote systems that are highly centralized (i.e., mainframe systems) and under their control, and they discourage or attempt to prohibit the use of microcomputers. If this is the reason for denying the use of microcomputers, it is a very poor reason—one that ultimately may not be in the best interests of the company.

The Company Acknowledges the Potential of Microcomputers, But Does Not Wish to Incur the Additional Necessary Costs for Training and Support Services

Training and support command significant resources and account for most of the operational costs of using microcomputers. If a company does not want to support such costs, it is justified in not acquiring and using microcomputers on those grounds alone.

The Company Is Concerned That, With the Rapid Changes in Computer Technology, Any Systems Acquired Now Could Soon Become Obsolete; They Would Prefer To Wait For What Is Coming Out Next

This reason is often given by companies that have not yet invested in any micro-computer technology, but the legitimacy of the reason is questionable. All such expenditures should be judged on the trade-off between expected benefits to be realized over a period of time and expected costs over that same period.

Looking at *currently* available options for current problems, a decision maker ought to choose the one that would provide the greatest benefits for a given cost. The decision maker who chooses to wait for something even better to come along will suffer the loss of all the benefits that could have been realized until that something better does come along (if indeed it ever does come along). There is also the very real likelihood that the "something better" may have a higher price tag.

Good managers know that today's problems demand today's solutions. Decisions are not necessarily made better by waiting for alternatives that have not yet been invented.

13.2 JUSTIFYING MICROCOMPUTER TECHNOLOGY

Justifying microcomputers is the same as justifying any corporate expenditure. It is expected that the return on the investment will exceed the investment itself. Unfortunately, it is not always easy to determine the return that microcomputers are presumed to provide. Many of the benefits are intangibles.

Some companies make no pretext at assessing the benefits of microcomputers. They are presumed to be cost effective. But it is a wise company that looks critically at the evidence and makes a determination about the past, current, and projected value of microcomputer systems to their own company. Such scrutiny may not be popular in a company where microcomputers have already made substantial inroads, but ultimately the value of microcomputer technology will need to be assessed, if only to determine how the company may profit by expanding its use.

If microcomputer technology is being used, but is not returning good value, the reasons need to be known so that corrective actions may be taken. Taking action may be as simple as acquiring new software or providing better user training.

13.3 POTENTIAL BENEFITS OF MICROCOMPUTER USE

Regardless of the way a justification is made, the actual or potential benefits need to be identified along with the possible liabilities and costs. Some of the major tangible and intangible benefits are listed next, followed by the potential liabilities and costs of microcomputer use.[1]

---

[1]*Tangible benefits* are defined as those that are measurable or easily expressed in quantitative terms. *Intangible benefits* are those that can be measured only with great difficulty or not at all.

Tangible Benefits

- New capabilities (e.g., spread-sheet analysis)
- Increased quality of work output
- Increased quantity of work output
- Increased task efficiency and accuracy
- Reduced worker hours (salary savings)
- Reduced clerical operations
- Reduction of paper work and paper handling
- Better control of inventory, schedules, and the like
- Quicker access to data and information
- Increased access to data processing
- Reduction of redundant data and file keeping
- Conservation of mainframe computer time and data storage

Intangible Benefits

- Increased data relevance
- Timely access to data
- Improved data formats and presentations
- Improved decision-making capabilities through modeling
- Greater user convenience in working with data
- Data-processing systems that are easier to use
- Greater user satisfaction[2]

Among the tangible benefits, increased capabilities, increased quality of work output, and increased quantity of work output are considered to be the most important. Many users, however, feel that, on an intuitive level, the intangible benefits are probably more important to most companies than are the tangible benefits.

13.4 LIABILITIES AND COSTS OF MICROCOMPUTER USE

Microcomputer systems also present liabilities at times, and they certainly incur costs. The following list suggests a few of the more common liabilities:

- Reduced employee morale: some employees refuse or resist contact with computers in any form; this presents a problem for the company if employees (particularly managers) are expected to work with microcomputers;

---

[2]The items in these two lists have been suggested by corporate microcomputer users and by managers of corporate microcomputer resources.

it also may generate resentment from employees who feel forced to work with computers.

- Loss of employee productivity while employees are learning to use the microcomputer and various software programs.
- Loss of employee productivity due to time spent "playing" or otherwise engaged in nonproductive microcomputer activities.
- Users require "outside" technical support such as training, programming, and technical assistance (otherwise, high-salaried manager/user time will be consumed inefficiently).
- Some users think that computers tend to increase their work loads.
- Some users think that their work is monitored more closely and that mistakes are more evident; that the use of computers makes them "look bad."
- The introduction of microcomputers (any computer) and automated systems changes the way things have always been done; procedures are changed; work is disrupted (at least for a period of time).
- Too much time is directed to working with microcomputers in lieu of doing other necessary work.
- If you provide some employees with microcomputers, others will want them (presumably whether they need them or not).

The loss of employee productivity while learning how to use microcomputers and the fact that users need outside technical support are among the most important liabilities. All these liabilities can be anticipated and dealt with "up front." None of these liabilities, at least by themselves, seem serious enough to override the benefits that accrue from microcomputer use.

The costs of microcomputer use are similar to costs incurred for other office technologies. They are emphatically not close to cost levels of mainframe computing. However, some companies, in their eagerness to justify the acquisition of microcomputer systems, tend to overlook or ignore some of the less obvious costs of microcomputing. The following list identifies a number of obvious system costs, as well as a few that are hidden and easily overlooked.

Microcomputer Systems Costs

Hardware

- The basic computer system consisting of the computer unit itself, the keyboard, monitor, disk drives, and printer
- Other monitors (graphics, color)
- Special graphics boards
- Memory (RAM) enhancement boards
- Cables (often sold separately)
- Printers (draft quality, letter quality, color)

- Graphics plotter
- Digitizers, mouse, light pens, joy sticks
- Modems
- Serial interface boards (often not included with the basic system)
- Special circuit board to connect to the mainframe
- Hard-disk drive unit (if not part of basic system)
- Hard-disk backup unit
- Networking circuit boards and cabling
- Electrical surge filter

Software

- Operating systems
- Software packages purchased off the shelf
- Consultation with software companies (information is usually free, but time spent by the user and long-distance telephone charges are not)
- Time spent finding, evaluating, and ordering software
- Time spent configuring or modifying new software
- Time spent learning how to use unfamiliar software
- Time spent designing, coding, and debugging user-created software
- Time spent learning how to write programs and to design programs that work

Supplies

- Diskettes
- Printer paper
- Printer ribbons and type fonts
- Disk storage boxes and storage cabinets
- Disk-head cleaning kits
- Antistatic spray
- Plotter pens, special paper, transparency film

Furniture

- Special keyboard-height computer desk
- Display monitor tilt/swivel stand
- Typing easel
- Special screen filter to control glare
- Locks and security devices

Installation, Setup, and Maintenance

• Special electrical wiring (necessary in some cases)
• Special cabling to the mainframe and networks
• Telephone connection or addition of data line
• Service contracts or outside repair fees
• Screwdrivers, pliers, and cable ties

Subscriber Fees and Publications

• Database subscriber fees
• Subscriptions to magazines and journals
• Membership fees to user groups

Training

• Training materials, manuals, and reference books
• Training courseware
• Keyboard templates
• Outside training seminars

Administrative

• Costs of evaluating the purchase request
• Costs of preparing the purchase and service contracts
• Miscellaneous telephone and travel expenses

Salaries

• User's time
• Clerical support and data entry services
• Programmer's time (if used)
• Technician's time (if used)
• Analyst's time (if used)
• Data processing manager and/or database managers' time (if used)

While not all these costs would be incurred for every user, they do represent real costs incurred in the process of making microcomputer systems operational. The greater the number of microcomputer users, the greater the costs will obviously be, although in some areas, such as user support and training, savings may be had through economies of scale.

When first purchasing microcomputer systems, there is a tendency to think that the hardware costs command the largest category of expenditures. For one or a few users who use their microcomputers infrequently, this may be true. But for larger numbers of users, the major expenditures will be in the category of salaries.

It may be argued that users' salaries would be paid irrespective of whether or not microcomputers were used. This is true, but the actual costs of the system must account for the loss of productivity of such salaries during the initial and subsequent learning hiatus.

Other salaries may also contribute to microcomputer system costs, such as the time spent by data-processing managers, database administrators, or other systems consultants when a microcomputer user wishes to access the mainframe and its data bases.

Where the data-processing staff supports microcomputer users, the creation or modification of software may consume substantial amounts of professional analyst and programmer time. The cost of software development for microcomputers done by in-house programming staff is just as costly as software developed for a large mainframe computer system.

The use of microcomputers may also stimulate new ways of carrying out operations and procedures. Their use may call for a system modification or conversion. While difficult to identify and document, systems conversions demand resources, if not in the development of new procedures, at least in a loss of productivity while others are learning to adjust to those changes.

13.5 BENEFITS VERSUS COSTS

The list of costs in the foregoing may be intimidating to those contemplating the use of microcomputers. They were not presented to intimidate but to suggest many of the real costs of microcomputer use. It is usually better to be aware of such costs before they are incurred rather than to be surprised at a later time.

It may seem, however, that the benefits of microcomputers could not outweigh the potential liabilities including costs. This can only be determined for each company on an individual basis. Within a given company, one application may be judged cost effective while another is not. The utility of any system must be determined within the context of company objectives, the operations necessary to achieve those objectives, and the alternatives available for carrying out necessary operations. These are all *organization specific*.

The real question is not "Can the company afford microcomputers?" but "Which of several competing alternative technologies (including manual systems) produces the most benefits for the least cost?"

If the preceding list of costs is found to be intimidating, it may be well to keep in mind that other alternative systems (including inefficient manual systems) have their costs too. It may also be helpful to remember that in the cost-benefit race, microcomputer systems have fared very well for many companies.

13.6 DECISION GUIDELINES

In the absence of hard data on benefits and costs, it is expected that most companies will make a "gut level" decision to use microcomputers. A few guidelines are presented here that may assist decision makers to focus their attention on important issues.

Guidelines for Assessing the Potential Value of Microcomputers

1. Identify exactly where the system is to be located, who will use it, and for what applications.
2. Identify whether the application is new or an existing application. If the application is new, identify how it contributes to company objectives. If it is an existing application, identify how the microcomputer will add value (i.e., accomplish that activity quicker, with greater accuracy, with less cost, with less trouble, etc.)
3. Determine whether or not the company has existing but underutilized resources for carrying out this application.
4. Determine who, other than the user(s) of the proposed system, may be affected by the use of the new system. Will it change how things are done? Will it change the direction or nature of work flow? Will it have effects across management lines?
5. Determine what will initially be purchased and what it will cost in direct dollars. Determine probable ongoing costs.
6. Determine expected long-term effects, such as the addition of future systems, hiring of staff, and expansion or enhancement of the initial system.

Should a company microcompute? That is a question each company must answer for itself. But every company should seriously investigate microcomputer technology as a means to

- Increase paperwork efficiency
- Increase office productivity
- Improve response to customers
- Improve decision making at all management levels
- Increase staff productivity without necessarily increasing staff
- Automate procedures that are currently done manually
- Ease access to existing corporate data
- Broaden use of new data-processing tools such as spreadsheet, word processing, and database management systems

13.7 MICROCOMPUTERS AND PRODUCTIVITY

Before leaving this chapter, a further word or two needs to be said about justifying microcomputer technology on the basis of increased corporate productivity. Microcomputer marketeers are well aware of the mounting pressures business managers are feeling in trying to deal with the information explosion. They are sensitive to the fact that corporate productivity is becoming more and more dependent on how information is handled internally, and that is why their advertising prose is sprinkled liberally with promises of increased productivity—if only you buy their product.

Their claims are *potentially* true, of course, but the introduction of a new technology, especially one that requires employees to master new skills and procedures, *does not automatically guarantee increased productivity*.

The purpose of microcomputers in business is to process data. And insofar as improved data processing contributes to either lowered operating costs or increased revenues, microcomputer technology will earn its keep. Like any other business technology, microcomputers must be expected to pay their own way by contributing directly to an increase in productivity. Microcomputers can and ought to be regarded as productivity-enhancing tools.

But even if a company could afford to suddenly equip all or most of its employees with microcomputers, there is no assurance that benefits would be forthcoming that would justify such a venture. Corporate productivity is dependent on more than just having the technology at hand.

To misunderstand this is to compromise the potential value to be realized by the use of any technology. A close look at productivity itself shows why. The formula for productivity is simple enough. It has not changed throughout history:

Right People + Right Working Conditions + Right Tools = Productivity

The formula says that productivity is the product of the right people, working under the right conditions, and equipped with the right tools and technologies that help them to do their jobs. Remove or compromise any one of these three essential factors—people, organizational conditions, or tools—and productivity is either not possible or severely constrained.

In most corporate settings, these three factors operate dynamically and interactively. A change in one causes or necessitates a change in the other. Like pieces in a puzzle, each of the three factors must achieve a "best fit" with each of the others.

As Figure 13.1 shows, the degree of fit or compatibility between people, working conditions, and tools establishes the *zone of productivity*. Increase the compatibility between these factors and the potential for productivity increases.

Just increasing any one factor in relation to the other two does not guarantee increased productivity. As Figure 13.2 shows, even though one factor is increased in magnitude, the zone of potential productivity does not necessarily increase.

It is only when all three factors are mutually compatible and complement each other, as in Figure 13.3, that the potential for productivity is at its greatest.

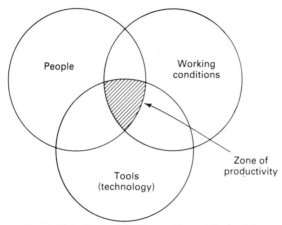

Figure 13.1   Productivity Factors: Zone of Productivity

Increasing one in magnitude without also increasing the "fit" of the others does little to foster increased productivity.

The key to improving productivity is to improve any or all three factors. If a production situation suffers for lack of the right people, then restaffing or training may provide the solution. If a production situation suffers from a lack of the right

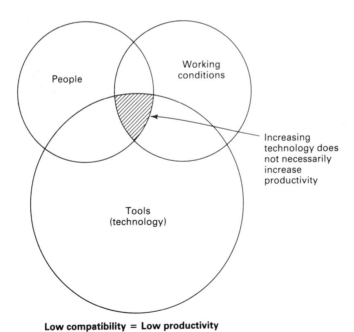

Low compatibility = Low productivity

Figure 13.2   Productivity Relationships: Low Productivity

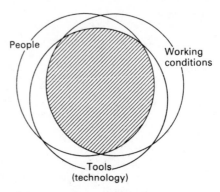

High compatibility = High productivity

Figure 13.3   Productivity Relationships: High Compatibility

working conditions, then a change in corporate climate, organization, policy, procedures, or working conditions may suffice. If a production situation suffers for lack of the right tools, then attention to providing useful, effective, and efficient tools is the answer.

Microcomputers are tools that, when used intelligently, contribute to increased business productivity. But even the best tools will fail if users are not knowledgeable, skilled, and motivated to use them in the most effective ways, and if organizational conditions are not in tune with independent, automated, and end-user operated data-processing and information retrieval systems. The productivity of microcomputers is dependent on more than just the presence of hardware and software alone.

When microcomputers contribute to corporate productivity over the long term, it will be because all three of these factors—people, working conditions, and the technology—have been viewed and managed holistically. Users will be knowledgeable and well trained, the corporate climate will encourage and support independent end-user data processing and access to data, and microcomputer hardware and software tools will be provided to whatever extent they are needed to assist in the work of the company.

14

Managing Microcomputer Resources

Small companies with few microcomputers will not find it necessary to manage microcomputer resources in any very formal way. Microcomputer users who use microcomputers only for budget preparation and for "what if" analysis may not need much assistance and can probably get along quite nicely with whatever information they can obtain from vendors or get casually from friends in the data-processing department.

But large organizations are beginning to see microcomputers as a growing and pervasive new technology. They recognize the necessity of supporting users as a way of getting maximum productivity and return on their investment. In response to users, they have organized formal support-service agencies within the company, and they are finding that some form of centralized coordination and management is necessary.

14.1 MANAGEMENT OF MICROCOMPUTER TECHNOLOGY

Over the years, corporations have learned a valuable lesson: *technological innovation*, as it applies to the operations of the company itself, requires strong management. This does not necessarily mean that new technology should be strongly controlled. Rather, it means that technology tends to "shake up" the way things have always been done. It stimulates change. Unless new technology is guided and supported in accord with the objectives of the company, some of those changes may lead to problems.

A prudent management response is to acknowledge that technology can potentially create problems as well as help solve them, and then to guide the use of the new technology through the development of policy and through organizational support.

There are numerous cases where technology has proved to be a mixed blessing. The automobile is a classic case, with its contribution to air pollution and the mortality rate. Fortunately, we learn to live with it. We manage.

Likewise, every information technology has created problems as well as solved them. Although we do not think of the typewriter, the telephone, or the photocopier as particularly troublesome, each of these technologies has in turn produced problems that had to be solved. If we have not suffered greatly with these technologies, it is because their invasion and subsequent corporate adaptation took place over a longer period of time.

The more recent introduction of computer technology has radically changed the way companies conduct their business. The advantages have been enormous and incalculable, but there have been (and still are) many problems attendant to the use of computers. Virtually everyone has felt the impact of computers, even though computer services themselves have been somewhat isolated and hidden away in corporate data-processing departments.

Now microcomputers appear to be having a similar impact, except that microcomputer technology, perhaps more than any previous technology, affects managers and other information workers directly.

It is a fair observation that once a technology of this type has been introduced, things change, and it is not possible to go back to the previous ways of doing things. We would not consider doing without the telephone, the copier, the typewriter, or the electronic calculator. Modern business operations are shaped by these technologies. We take them for granted. Yet the microcomputer promises to replace or assimilate every single one of these individual technologies. Such a powerful technology cannot help but have powerful effects. Perhaps it, too, will soon be taken for granted. In the meantime, managers will have to confront a number of problems, unless such problems can be anticipated and handled before they have a chance to occur.

14.2 THE MANAGEMENT AGENDA

The first step in managing a new technology is to acknowledge its potential for creating problems. The second step is to take whatever actions are necessary to prevent those potential problems from becoming real ones. Managers should initially address these questions:

- What plan should the company follow to ensure the best outcome?
- Who should manage the company microcomputers?
- What is the best approach to managing both users and resources?
- How can management remain accountable?

14.3 PLANNING FOR THE BEST OUTCOME

The first step in planning is to take stock of the current situation. This is done by answering four questions:

- Where are we at? What is happening right now that commands our attention?
- How did we get here? What events or forces led us to this situation?
- Where do we want to be? What are the goals and objectives to be realized at some future date?
- How are we going to get there? What resources, know-how, and techniques are at our disposal?

Any company planning and developing microcomputer resources must at some point either formally or informally address each of these four questions. The first two questions require answers that are specific to an individual company. They provide background and perspective to the introduction of microcomputer technology. Usually, they focus on problems that the company has had to deal with in the past or with the company's attempt to seize an opportunity (perhaps for improved productivity). The answers may also reveal both short- and long-term problems that will need to be resolved.

The second two questions address the real planning issues. Answers to these two questions will form the *plan of action*. They should be answered by those who are in a position to answer resource and policy questions. With feet on the ground and a clear vision of what really needs to be accomplished, the management of microcomputer resources can move steadily ahead.

14.4 WHO SHOULD MANAGE?

Before the management of microcomputer resources can proceed very far, someone must be put in charge. Someone must be delegated the authority to carry out whatever directives, policies, and plans are set forth by upper-level managers. Deciding "who should manage the microcomputers" should not be accomplished by default, nor should the decision be delegated too far down the corporate ladder. To do so is a mistake from which it may be very difficult, if not impossible, to recover.

Who should manage the microcomputers? Who owns them? Who is in the best position, in terms of knowledge, to know how to best support and develop microcomputer resources? Who is managing now? Is that management effective? Is such management in the best interests of the company over the long run?

These are not easy questions to answer. But the answers will set the style and nature of microcomputer resource management for a time to come. These questions need carefully considered answers, perhaps more than they need expedient ones. Obviously, different companies will answer these questions in different ways.

When it comes to managing microcomputers, there are two schools of thought. The first school is that the microcomputer manager ought to be someone with a strong formal data-processing background, someone who understands the technical aspects of microcomputers.

The second school is that the microcomputer manager ought to be someone with a strong management background, someone who has firsthand experience with the kinds of business problems and decisions that will be supported by microcomputer technology. The differences between these two schools of thought are more philosophical than substantive. A case can be made for either camp.

The strengths that favor candidates from data processing are that they have a background in information and data processing, they understand the technical side of computer hardware, they understand the technical side of software and programming, and they may already be involved with microcomputer and other types of end-user systems.

On the negative side, candidates from a professional data-processing background may be perceived as being too technically oriented and therefore less able to perceive problems from the perspective of the nontechnically oriented user. They may be seen as having too much loyalty to the mainframe computer system and are therefore suspect in not giving appropriate attention and priority to microcomputer users.

The strengths and weaknesses of candidates outside data processing are less clear. Candidates might be considered who have a strong belief in the use of microcomputers as information-processing tools, those who are microcomputer users themselves, those who have a strong allegiance to microcomputer users, and so on.

It might be argued that any manager of microcomputer resources ought have a strong management background not only so that they can be effective managers of microcomputer resources, but also so that microcomputing can be seen from the perspective of management decision making and operations. It also could be argued that, whatever the background, candidates for this manager position should be well grounded in data processing and information-systems fundamentals. Perhaps in addition to data processing, they should also strongly believe in the use of microcomputers, and they should be able to quickly perceive the problems of potential users and be able to recommend specific microcomputer applications solutions. They should be very people oriented and feel comfortable in approaching all types of users at all levels of use within the company.

While a number of corporate microcomputer resource managers have been chosen because of their technical knowledge of microcomputers, the primary role of most successful corporate microcomputer managers is not that of the technical expert. Such expertise is needed, of course, but the manager needs to function as an advocate and a change agent for this technology, and to give guidance and direction to other staff members, who in turn provide technical assistance, training, and other support services.

In the final analysis, the choice of a manager should not be made on the basis of affiliation or nonaffiliation with the data-processing department. It should be a choice made after reviewing the qualifications of each candidate for the position after it has been determined what resources are to be managed and after it is known what type of staff support the manager can expect to manage. The necessary qualifications for a manager of a staff of one will be very different from a manager of a staff of several microcomputer support specialists.

In creating a microcomputer resource manager position, some consideration should be given to the appropriate organizational level of that position. While it is important that microcomputer support services be organized and developed to support all users, it is especially important that they be organized to serve mid- and upper-level managers since they are very much a manager's tool. The microcomputer resource manager may be more effective when the management position level is close to the position level of the managers being served. A microcomputer support person ranking considerably below the level of microcomputer users would likely not be as effective as one at or near the level of users.

14.5 MANAGEMENT APPROACHES

The successful introduction of microcomputer technology and the ability to sustain user productivity will depend on the relationship established between users and those who support their use. Therefore, the management approach taken is critical.

What kind of management is called for? Other than clerical staff, microcomputers are going to be used by managers or other highly placed professionals who are typically self-starters, self-directed, and business professionals who know what they want to accomplish. As a group, they do not need much outside direction and they generally will not tolerate arbitrarily imposed controls. They need a high degree of access to services without many rules and restraints. They will not take kindly to someone outside their own department dictating the how-to's, when-to's, or why-to's of microcomputer use.

If they are not using a microcomputer, they certainly will not want anyone telling them they must. If they are already using a microcomputer, they will have invested considerable time, effort, and ego in learning how to make it work. If they have done this independently, they are going to be fairly aggressive in maintaining this independence.

In all likelihood, they will have developed a loyalty to a particular brand or model of hardware and software. They will resist any externally imposed "standards" unless those standards just happen to agree with their own biases.

Obviously, a more effective management approach is going to be one that respects the feelings of users, approaches them with extreme tact, and, in general, is in no way heavy handed.

The other side of the management issue is that without some kind of centralized force working for the interests of the company as a whole, resources may be wasted, misused, or underutilized. A major problem that has arisen is a lack of formal guidelines for users and appropriate standards. Purchases made without guidance have often resulted in an incompatible mixture of hardware and software. A centralized effort to consolidate purchases and to maximize resources results in greater output for microcomputer expenditures. For example, a few dollars doled out to individual users for training might not result in very much training. But those same few dollars pooled into a training fund might purchase training seminars for a large number of users.

The centralized coordination of resource expenditures is one of the strongest justifications for centralized management. At a certain point, users ought not to be left only to their own resources. They should be given support, guidance, and, in the best interests of the company, some framework of policy restraints.

What is the answer, then? How can two seemingly opposite needs be reconciled? Users are obviously very decentralized and management, by definition, is a centralizing force. Since microcomputer use is driven to a large degree by individual user initiative, no good end would come from totally centralizing microcomputer management. If use is to be encouraged and sustained, it is necessary that microcomputers be managed in such a way that initiative is not quashed.

One very effective management approach is *to minimize control over microcomputer users and to maximize the support given to them.* If users primarily view microcomputer management as an organizational service designed to support them in acquiring systems and resolving difficulties, the few policies and procedures necessary for maintaining some kinds of control will be accepted as a necessary trade-off. This strategy of decentralized utilization coupled with centralized control and support can serve as a system of checks and balances to keep things working effectively and harmoniously.

It is also a good idea to involve existing microcomputer users (the old guard) in the formulation of policies that will govern microcomputer use. Any particularly constraining policies will be more readily accepted if both users and policymakers can share their concerns and work out policies that are mutually acceptable. It is important that users at all levels recognize that they and high-level managers are on the same side and have common goals in the use and support of microcomputers. Of course, such involvement of users in helping to shape policy must be perceived as an honest effort to include them in working out the rules, and not as mere tokenism.

14.6 LONG-TERM ACCOUNTABILITY

Even if microcomputers are just being introduced into a corporate environment, it is not too early for managers to think about their long-term impact. If, over the long term, microcomputer use is successful, there will be no lack of persons to take the credit. If it is less than successful or becomes problematic, it will likely be the manager of these resources who will take the blame. Wise managers plan for either contingency by aggressively tracking and documenting the progress of microcomputer integration into their company's day-to-day operations.

Periodic management reviews are required in most organizations, and it behooves the microcomputer resource manager to anticipate such reviews and to plan for them well in advance. The documentation of achievements should not be difficult during the initial months of microcomputer use.

If microcomputer technology is successful, the evidence will be everywhere. Hardware will be prominently displayed in offices and users will frequently be seen working at the consoles. There will be a whole new subculture of users speaking the language, sharing information, and waxing enthusiastic about this or that new piece of hardware or software.

At a later time, such evidence may be less obvious. It is at this point that the tough questions are going to be asked by upper-level management—questions such as, What are we getting in return for all the dollars we have spent on microcomputers?, Wouldn't we have been better off to have invested in a broader mainframe network?, or Can't we begin cutting back on the purchase of microcomputers and the support services budget?

For upper-level management, these are appropriate questions to be asking at this stage, even in the face of what may seem overwhelming success with the use of microcomputers. The wise resource manager will have anticipated such questions and will be prepared to provide solid answers.

Complete answers cannot be anticipated ahead of an actual management review, but the time for anticipating such questions and the data necessary to support the answers to such questions is during the earliest stages of adoption and use. *It is prudent for microcomputer managers to start structuring their own periodic reviews and accountability from day one.*

They should anticipate the significant outcomes expected at each stage (those expected to be interpreted by upper-level managers as significant), gather supporting documentation and relevant data, and then be prepared to present such documentation when such a report is requested or when it is otherwise appropriate to do so. (Reports may be timed to coincide with the routine processes of corporate planning or strategically submitted a short time before negotiations on next year's budget.)

A year-end report or impact assessment report does not need to be too extensive, but it does need to be complete and absolutely truthful. Both the good and the bad must be told. Anything less than complete candor will cast a veil of suspicion on the whole document and perhaps on the motives of the manager submitting the report.

The contents and format of a year-end report should minimally contain the objectives, the activities undertaken, and the outcomes or results of these activities. An outline of such a study is presented in Appendix B.

Another useful management tool is the *impact study*. An impact study is done once to document how microcomputers have affected users, specific departments, and the company as a whole. It is usually done six to eighteen months after the company has made a commitment and significant resources have been expended. The impact study details the benefits that have been achieved and the problems that have occurred as a result of the new program since its beginning.

The impact study addresses questions that upper-level managers will want to know:

- What have we done?
- What were the results?
- What has it cost us?
- What did we get for our money?

A more detailed outline of an impact study is presented in Appendix C.

An impact study is very difficult to do if it has not been planned well in advance and if supporting data have not been gathered from the beginning of the program. Once data-collection opportunities are missed, they usually cannot be recaptured.

An impact study is done primarily to document the *success* of a unique activity or project. It is done to satisfy upper-managers that their decision to support such an activity was a correct one. Whether solicited by upper-level managers or not, an impact study, if done well and presented at the right time, can have a very salutary effect on the program, on participants, on management, and, of course, on all who have been instrumental in making the program a success.

The process of doing an impact study also is a valuable management exercise. It forces the manager to focus on salient management issues, it forces the collection of meaningful data and factual evidence, it puts the manager in touch with users, and it focuses attention on past successes, current problems, and future directions that might otherwise go unnoticed.

Long-term planning is still another important accountability tool. Unlike the impact study, which may be done once in the early, start-up stages of corporate microcomputer use, long-term planning should be done every year. It is often combined with an end-of-year report to provide a planning document that assesses past objectives and accomplishments and sets new objectives for the future. A microcomputer resource manager should create a long-term plan and then focus resources and efforts on carrying out that plan successfully.

It is absolutely essential that such a plan solicit and incorporate the ideas of users and other managers. The best long-range plans for service organizations are those produced in collaboration with consumers of the services. Not only will such collaboration provide useful insight and a sense of priorities, but it will also generate support and enthusiasm from the individuals who feel they have a vested interest in the continuing success of the support organization.

An effective long-range plan does not have to be elaborate or voluminous (shorter documents are more likely to be read anyway), but the plan should address the following questions:

- What are our *problems*?
- What can we *do* about them?
- What *opportunities* might we anticipate?
- How can we take advantage of these opportunities?
- What are the *priorities?* What needs attention first?
- What specifically *should happen* by some future date?
- What *resources* do we need to make these things happen?

Long-range plans typically anticipate events and set objectives for periods of three to five years into the future. In a fast-paced and rapidly changing environment, it may be difficult to anticipate the values, company objectives, and conditions which may exist that far into the future. Microcomputer technology and the company's use of microcomputers may look very different in five years. This does not invalidate long-range microcomputer resource planning, but it does make any plans less certain and more subject to revision.

A useful planning strategy is to make short and intermediate plans as well as long-term ones. A comprehensive plan might set objectives for three periods of time:

- Short-term objectives (to be accomplished over a 1- to 6-month period)
- Intermediate-term objectives (to be accomplished over a 6- to 18-month period)
- Long-term objectives (to be accomplished over a 2- to 5-year period)

The use of year-end reviews, impact studies, and long-range planning documents should make the management of microcomputer resources easier by increasing the credibility of the support service organization and by presenting a positive and beneficial picture of the organization to upper-level managers and users alike.

There is little question that microcomputer technology (or some advanced form of it) will be a central and essential adjunct to corporate business activities within a very few years. Even though the microcomputer movement is largely user driven and user oriented, the success of microcomputers in the corporate environment will not come about through the users alone acting on their own behalf. How well microcomputer resources are used, how quickly and smoothly their use is integrated and normalized into the mainstream, and how effective users become will surely be a function of how well they are managed.

15

Formulating Microcomputer Policy

The need for corporate policy controls on microcomputer use is no less acute than for other business activities. The independent nature of microcomputer use tends to make each user and system a miniature data-processing domain unto itself. Obviously, dozens (or perhaps hundreds) of these independent domains are not in the best interests of company-wide data and information management. Corporate microcomputer users need to be given the boundaries and conditions of acceptable use early in the game.

Microcomputer policy is not only necessary, it is essential to establish workable and efficient microcomputer-based information systems. Companies who invest heavily in microcomputer technology should issue a policy manual (even a preliminary one) as soon as it is possible to do so. An ounce of policy at the earliest stages of microcomputer use may be worth far more than a pound of management intervention after several months have passed and users and departments begin working by their own rules. Control, once lost, is very hard to regain.

15.1 THE NATURE OF POLICY

What is policy? *A policy is fundamentally a statement of a position taken by management on a particular issue.* Corporate policy statements are intended to serve as guides to employees. They are, in their simplest form, a description of how the company would like employees to act in particular circumstances and situations. They guide future actions and decisions.

A policy is really a corporate rule—a "do" or a "don't." It may be blunt, as in "Employees will not remove microcomputer hardware, software, or disks containing corporate information and data from the premises." Or it may be subtle, as in the statement "Users are encouraged to consult with the Microcomputer Resource Manager before purchasing hardware and software." In this case the language is *subtle* because the word "encouraged" may be interpreted by upper-level managers to mean "required."

A company's policies may be in written form or they may be in unwritten form, but in either form they must be known to employees before they can be observed.[1] A good case can be made for having policies in a written form. (As someone has observed, oral policies, like oral contracts, are not worth the paper they are written on!) In written form, policies may be easily and uniformly distributed, and they are much more likely to be observed and uncontested.

15.2 MICROCOMPUTER POLICY ISSUES

At the invitation of the author, a number of corporate microcomputer users and managers were asked to share some of the problems that arise because of microcomputer use in their companies, and to describe either the policies that had been created to deal with these problems or policies that they feel should be created.

The fifty or so individuals asked to share this information came from a variety of both large and small corporate settings, and they collectively represented diverse geographical areas.[2] Despite their business and geographical diversity, the same concerns regarding corporate microcomputer use tended to surface.

The contributor's comments about corporate microcomputer problems and policies were compiled into a large list. This list was then reduced by eliminating redundancies and by looking for a single set of policy issues. To achieve some degree of uniformity, the comments were rephrased as policy questions.

The result is a list of questions that might be asked by managers in anticipation of their own companies' concerns and as a precursor to the formulation of

---

[1]Most established companies have any number of unwritten policies (rules, regulations, codes of conduct) that are generally known and observed by employees. Often such policies refer to modes of acceptable dress, absenteeism, work hours, the use of profanity, fraternization, and other forms of social conduct. Such policies are part of the "corporate culture" and are passed from employee-to-employee by word of mouth.

[2]Most of the respondents were microcomputer users themselves, but in most cases they had managerial responsibilities related to corporate microcomputer use. Respondents included in the group came from Alabama, Alaska, California, Colorado, Maine, and North Carolina.

corporate microcomputer policy. The objective was to create a "core set" of policy questions from which corporate policymakers could work to create the policy framework for employee involvement with microcomputer resources.

The questions seem to fall naturally into one of four related categories. They are therefore presented in four groupings.

Group 1

The first group of policy issues *focuses on justifying microcomputer applications and uses, controlling unrestrained purchases, dealing with the problems of hardware and software compatibility, and addressing the issues of standardization.*

Issue: authorized microcomputer applications

- Who should/should not use microcomputers?
- What reasons justify acquisition of hardware and software?
- What are the legitimate applications for the company?

Issue: reviewing/screening purchase requests

- Should purchase requests be reviewed by a central authority?
- Who should determine who gets and who does not get a microcomputer?

Issue: hardware standards

- What kinds of microcomputers should the company allow?
- Should the company adopt a standard make and model?
- If a standard is adopted, what should those standards be? Who should decide?
- Should the company sponsor hardware evaluations? Provide test models?

Issue: software standards

- What restrictions should the company place on software purchases?
- Should the company adopt standard software packages?
- If a standard is adopted, what should those standards be? Who should decide?
- Should the company sponsor software evaluations before adopting a standard?

Issue: systems compatibility

- How necessary is it to insist on compatibility?
- How should the company define compatibility?
- How will noncompatibility affect future data sharing? Networking? Resource management? Training?
- What data formats are standard? Is one better than another?

These are all concerns of a company that suddenly realizes something major is happening over which it has too little knowledge and control. When management raises these questions it is saying, "Hold on. What's going on here with micro-computers? Are we on the right track? Let's pause a bit, take stock, reevaluate the situation, and set some directions."

Group 2

The second group of issues deals with concerns about company risk. They *focus on concerns for the use of existing programming resources, on the need to exert professional standards on users who are developing software, and on the security and integrity of the corporate databases.*

Issue: software development

- Should in-house software development be permitted? Encouraged? Supported?
- What are the cost trade-offs between commercial off-the-shelf software and custom-designed software?
- Should professional programming staff be provided? Or should software development be limited only to programs that users themselves create?
- Should the use of data-processing staff programmers be allowed? If allowed, monitored? Who should control access to programmers' time?
- What are the real costs of user-developed software?
- If users develop software on company time, who owns it?
- Should user-developed software be available to others?
- What happens to such software when the user/developer leaves the company or moves to another position?
- Should user/developers be required to provide user guides and documentation? Copies of their programs and data files? Source listings of their programs?
- Should technical programming standards be imposed on user/developers?

Issue: company data security/database integrity

- How can the company protect itself against user/developer programming errors (especially when critical decisions may be made on data obtained from these programs)?
- What steps need to be taken to protect data confidentiality?
- Who ought to be allowed to connect their microcomputer to the corporate computers and databases?
- Should users be allowed to up-load data into mainframe computer files as well as down-load data from mainframe computer files?

Issue: user data security/recovery

- What needs to be done to ensure that microcomputer users will not lose their own data and programs?
- What provisions need to be made for backups and recovery after floppy disks are damaged or files are mistakenly erased?
- Are user's data files personal property or company property?

Issue: networking/data communications

- Should microcomputer networking be permitted? Encouraged?
- What should be the relationship between microcomputer users and the mainframe systems?
- Who should be equipped for data communications? Does it matter? What justifies the additional expenditures?

Issue: copyright infringement

- Where does the company stand on copyright violations and software piracy by employees?
- What is the company's exposure to litigation when employees make unauthorized copies of software?
- How can software copying be policed? Whose responsibility should it be?
- What should happen if copyright violations are discovered?
- Should the company arrange for multiuser licenses from software companies?

Issue: physical security

- What are the risks of loss, damage, and theft?
- Who "owns" the hardware and software? Departments?
- Who should manage the microcomputer inventory?

Issue: off-site use

- Should users be permitted to take computers home with them?
- When is off-site use justified? Who should authorize it?
- What are the potential benefits of off-site use? What are the potential liabilities?
- Will the company's insurance cover off-site use?
- What is the employee's liability?

These are concerns that very likely are raised by data-processing managers and database administrators, professionals who have trodden this same policy ground as it relates to the mainframe computer environment. This group of questions acknowledges the concern that the use of microcomputers for some applications entails risks for the company and that steps need to be taken to lessen those risks.

Group 3

The third group of concerns are for the welfare of the users themselves (and ultimately the company). *The focus is on what help and assistance users may need and what support services the company ought to feel obligated to provide in return for user success and productivity.*

Issue: user support services

- What are the expected needs of users? What support will they require?
- What support services would best serve the interests of the company?
- Who should provide such services?

Issue: centralized purchasing

- What controls should be placed on hardware and software purchases?
- Should purchases be handled centrally through a coordinating office or independently by user's departments?
- Should the company seek to develop a long-term relationship with vendors?
- How important is the vendor relationship as it applies to microcomputers?

Issue: user training

- What training is necessary? Can users "go it alone"?
- What is the best way to get users up to speed?
- Who should provide training? Individual departments? The training department? Data processing? Microcomputer support services? Outside vendors?

Issue: technical support

- What technical support is needed?
- Who should provide technical assistance such as equipment setup, hook-ups, and installation of new components?
- What repairs should be handled in-house? Who should do them?
- Should service contracts be purchased for microcomputers?
- If so, should those be on-site or carry-in?
- Who should manage and handle service contracts?

These concerns manifest recognition that microcomputers are a good thing and that users not only *should* be provided with appropriate support, but they *must* be provided with appropriate support if the potential for microcomputer technology is to be realized.

Group 4

The fourth, and last, group of concerns *deals with the organization of support services as well as the management of microcomputer resources on a day-to-day basis and over the long term.*

Issue: company goals for microcomputer use

- What are the company's goals in permitting/supporting/encouraging micro-computer use?
- What is the company's stake in microcomputers? What is the expected payoff?
- Are company objectives congruent or at odds with user objectives?

Issue: long-term planning

- Is long-term planning necessary? Desirable?
- Who ought to do it?
- How do microcomputers figure into the long-term plans for corporate information systems?

Issue: management accountability

- Is microcomputer use an individual, departmental, or company-wide responsibility?
- To whom should microcomputer users be accountable?
- What ought to be managed? Applications? Purchases? Support services? User accountability?

Issue: support services management

- Should microcomputer support be centralized? Decentralized within departments?
- If centralized, who should do it?
- What ought to be the primary role of such support services: control or service?

Issue: budget requirements

- What are the budget requirements for microcomputers individually? Collectively?
- What staffing is necessary?
- What facilities are necessary?
- What hardware? Software? Equipment? Operating expenses?
- Who is going to pay for it?

These concerns are those of a company that has made the commitment to developing microcomputer resources in a responsible way.

In some ways, these concerns are a natural evolution of a company's adoption of this new technology. Management's initial concerns are for exercising restraint and keeping things under control. At a later time, they are for protecting the company's existing data and information resources. Still later, the concerns turn toward the need to support users. And, finally, at the most mature stage of adoption, they focus on management itself over the long term.

These four groups represent specific areas of concern to different persons in the company. Policy issues may also be divided into two general groups according to who will be guided and directed by new policies: the microcomputer users and microcomputer resource managers.

15.3 FORMULATING POLICY STATEMENTS

The policy issues listed are just that—*policy issues.* In the form of questions, they only serve to stimulate the thinking of policy makers about what issues are relevant for their company and what position they may want their company to take. Once an issue has been identified as relevant to a company, a policy position still must be determined and the policy statement written.

Policy statements come in all shapes and forms. The simplest is simply a list of "do's" and "don'ts." While brief and to the point, such lists seem "bossy." They usually do not convey the company's thinking or rationale for instituting a given rule. They sound dictatorial and may very likely spark resentment.

It is an unfortunate failing of many company policy statements that they dictate a course of action but not the reasons that originally justified that course of action. As conditions change, a course of action appropriate at an earlier time may not remain the best course of action at a subsequent time. Employees find themselves in a position of having to observe a policy that is no longer valid (often the case in large bureaucratic organizations) or in a position of ignoring a policy (at the risk of possible bad consequences to themselves) that they know no longer makes sense. In the absence of the original reasons that prompted the formulation of a policy, it is very difficult for either employees or managers to judge a policy's continued usefulness.

The solution to this problem is to create a policy form that also provides the background information or reasons that led to the formulation of the particular policy in the first place. Then the policy, if it is questioned, can be reviewed and revalidated very quickly. The background only needs to be a simple narrative explaining the reasons and rationale that logically lead to a sanctioned course of action. A *because/therefore* model may be used to structure the logic. The model looks like this:

Because . . .
    reason
    reason
    reason
    etc.
Therefore . . .
    course of action
    course of action
    etc.

Here is an example of a policy's contents put together over this model policy skeleton:

Background:
    Because . . .
        long-distance is costly
        outside lines are overused
Policy Statement:
    Therefore . . .
        1. don't use microcomputers for data communications to other company locations.
        2. do use the corporate mainframe data-communications network.
        3. do use microcomputer data communications to access external databases and data services.

In this skeleton policy, the basic contents of the policy are laid out. It is clear what courses of action the company does and does not want employees to follow. The reasons for this policy are also clear—to reduce long-distance tolls and to relieve traffic on outside lines.

The logic, at least from the company's standpoint, is impeccable. If at a later time this policy is questioned, it is a simple matter to identify and validate the original reasons. Such a policy form is (to use the microcomputer vernacular) *user friendly*.

With the policy content clearly outlined, a more presentable version can be written. Although there really is nothing wrong with the readability of the original version, a "cleaned up" version might read as follows:

Policy Issue: Microcomputer Data Communications

Policy Background:
Long-distance telephone service costs are a source of concern to the company. It is necessary to reduce these costs where possible.
Also, outside lines are currently being used to capacity. It is necessary to conserve the use of outside lines by restricting use wherever possible.

Policy Statement:
Therefore, the company is enacting the following policies:
1. Microcomputer users should not use outside lines for microcomputer-based data communications (except as described in #3 below).
2. Whenever possible, the existing corporate mainframe computer network should be used for data communications.
3. Microcomputer users may use outside lines for data communications to access external databases and data services that are otherwise not accessible by the corporate mainframe data-communications network.

This version maintains the logic and the content of the earlier skeleton version, but the narrative has been fleshed out and the tone, while still businesslike, is softer and less "bossy." Note also that this final policy format is composed of three parts: (1) a policy issue name, (2) a policy background narrative, and (3) a policy statement narrative. The complete policy format model can be schematically shown as follows:

Policy Issue: [Suitable name]

Policy Background:
   [Narrative of reasons:
      Because . . .
        reason
        reason
        etc.]

Policy Statement:
   [Narrative of the policy itself:
      Therefore . . .
        course of action
        course of action
        etc.]

This policy format and a two-stage approach to writing policies is recommended. In the first stage, the policy writer succinctly identifies the *courses of action* to be required and the *reasons justifying these actions*. In other words, a *logical framework* for the policy is created. In the second stage, the writer improves the prose to make it communicate clearly and selects wording that will make the overall tone of the policy statement more friendly and less threatening to the "consumer."

15.4 SAMPLE POLICY STATEMENTS

A few examples of policy statements are presented next. These examples are intended only to serve as a guide for policymakers. Readers should feel free to adapt the ideas and modify the language in these examples in any way they find useful.[3]

Policy Issue: Authorized Microcomputer Applications

Policy background:

The company recognizes the use of microcomputer technology as a business tool to provide special computing and data-processing applications and capabilities. The microcomputer provides unexcelled utility in performing certain business and management operations. However, the microcomputer has diverse applications, not all of which are authorized as legitimate company applications.

Policy statement:

Employees should use microcomputers only for authorized applications. Unauthorized applications include playing games (except during nonbusiness hours) and writing software for commercial or personal use. Authorized applications are those that have been approved for specific job tasks by department supervisors and managers.

Policy Issue: Reviewing/Screening Purchase Requests

Policy background:

The company has a vested interest in the use of microcomputer technology and therefore takes a strong interest in all proposed new applications.

The company must ensure that microcomputer technology is not misused, that hardware and software are purchased with consideration of compatibility both

---

[3]The policy statements are provided as examples and suggestions. It is not the author's purpose to dictate microcomputer policy for any company. Every company should want to assess its own microcomputer resource situation and formulate policy appropriate to its own particular circumstances.

for current applications as well as for future networking and data sharing, and that options are considered in the assembly of a microcomputer system.

Policy statement:

The company therefore requires the following:

1. The request for purchase of new microcomputer hardware and software will be reviewed prior to approval for purchase by a designated review committee. The committee will make its recommendation to the budget director of the department making the request.

2. The review committee will establish guidelines to ensure that hardware and software purchases meet standards for compatibility.

3. The committee will determine the legitimacy of the proposed microcomputer application and will consult with the person making the request to ensure that other hardware and software options have been considered and that the proposed system configuration will achieve the proposed objectives.

Policy Issue: Microcomputer Vendor Relationships

Policy background:

The company recognizes that because of the nature of microcomputer marketing and sales, the relationship between the purchasing company and the vendor is important. The company seeks to establish such relationships with vendors that will ensure negotiation of the lowest costs for hardware and software and will provide required after-the-sale services and support.

Policy statement:

The company therefore requires the following:

1. All official and contractually binding communications with vendors will be made by designated company purchase agents, not by individual employees unless given specific authority to do so.

2. Employees contacting vendors for specific information should not discuss specific prices nor after-the-sale support.

Policy Issue: Company Data Security

Policy background:

The microcomputer provides an additional route of access to the company mainframe computer and databases. While it is desirable and convenient for certain company employees to access the mainframe computer and databases, it also creates a concern for data security and integrity of company data.

Policy statement:

The company therefore requires the following:

1. No access can be made to the mainframe computer or databases without specific authorization of the director of data processing.

2. Users must justify access to specific corporate files, and they will only be permitted access to those files where a specific need is demonstrated. Actual unauthorized access or attempted unauthorized access to company data files will be considered a serious company offense.

3. All microcomputer-to-mainframe computer hookups must be done only by designated technical staff.

4. All access by microcomputers will be limited to down-loading of files and data from the mainframe system to the microcomputer system. Up-loading may only be accomplished where the system operates in full emulation of a dedicated system terminal. In no case should access be made such that existing data-checking and editing provisions are avoided.

Policy Issue: Proprietary Software Rights

Policy background:

It is inevitable and desirable that employees create their own programs for special applications when commercially available software is not available. Because such software is developed using company resources, it is a company investment and needs to be protected as such.

Policy statement:

Therefore, the company requires the following:

1. All software developed by employees on company time or using company resources is considered company property. The company claims all proprietary rights as a condition of employment.

2. Users/developers must provide working copies of programs they have developed to the manager of microcomputer resources along with written documentation and source code listings.

3. Users/developers must surrender all copies and related materials upon termination or transfer to another department.

Policy Issue: Copyright Infringement

Policy background:

Microcomputer software is physically easy to copy, although in most cases it is illegal to do so. All commercial software may be assumed to be copyrighted and under the full protection of the copyright law. Commercially available software is licensed for a single user and/or microcomputer system. Some software publishers do provide special multiuser license arrangements, but it cannot be assumed that the company has made such arrangements.

Copying software for personal use or for use by other users even within the company is considered a copyright violation. Illegal copying by employees may expose the company to litigation.

Policy statement:

Therefore, the company requires the following:

1. No employee shall make a copy of copyrighted software for personal or for company use if that copy is not permitted by the licensing agreement. (Single working or backup copies are usually permitted, but the specific license agreement must be consulted before copying.)

2. All copies of software that are authorized under a negotiated multiple-user arrangement will be made and distributed to users by designated microcomputer support service personnel.

Policy Issue: Off-site Use

Policy background:

It is generally assumed that microcomputers will be used by employees within the company on company grounds. Because of the microcomputer's relative portability, it is expected that on specific occasions microcomputers will be used off site in the field, on trips to other cities and locations, and at the employee's home. Such use, while desirable in approved situations, increases the company's risk of loss, damage, and theft. Necessary precautions need to be taken.

Policy statement:

1. Off-site use will be done only with specific written permission in the form of a memo by the budget director of the department in which the microcomputer is normally housed. The memo must indicate the application, give the reasons justifying off-site use, list all hardware, software, and other items being taken along with their serial numbers, and give the planned date of return.

2. Microcomputer off-site use is not to be authorized if the absence of that system would deprive other users in a significant way.

3. Employees using company equipment and resources off site are expected to exercise due care and caution to prevent damage, loss, or theft. Under certain circumstances, the employee may be asked to assume full liability for loss, damage, or theft of a system.

Policy Issue: Support-services Management

Policy background:

The earliest company use of microcomputers involved few systems and users who required little in the way of support services. However, with the growth of microcomputer use, many users will need additional support and training services. It is appropriate for the company to assume a responsibility for providing such services in an organized and coordinated way.

The company also has vested interest in the successful use of microcomputer technology and requires the management of these resources to achieve specific long-term objectives.

Policy statement:

The company therefore establishes and requires the following:

1. A centralized unit to be organized and charged with these specific responsibilities:

A. To review systems purchase requests.

B. To organize and provide microcomputer support services to employees in the areas of hardware selection, software selection, systems operations training, repair and technical assistance, and such other services as may be necessary and useful to ensure appropriate and competent use of microcomputer technology.

C. To communicate microcomputer use policies to employees.

D. To establish and maintain a user's library of software, documentation, and other related technical and educational materials.

E To promote the use of microcomputer technology throughout the company.

15.5 COMMUNICATING POLICY TO MICROCOMPUTER USERS

Policy statements can be an extremely effective management tool for controlling and guiding employee behavior, but they are only effective if employees know they exist, read them, and understand what is really wanted by those who formulated the policy.[4] If policies are to be effective, they must be made public.

The methods used to communicate policy are every bit as important as the content itself. If policy statements are uncirculated or are poorly printed or are written in abstract and legalistic jargon, chances are that few employees will read them. *How* policy statements are communicated is critical.

---

[4]Employees are often unaware that particular policies exist. Policy statements typically are treated as semiprivate documents to be circulated only to managers and supervisors who then file or place them into three-ring binders along with other obscure and equally inaccessible policy statements.

After policies have been formulated and approved by management, it may be useful to publish a microcomputer user's handbook designed to capture existing and potential users' attention and to divulge relevant information about microcomputers and their use in the company. Such a document should be freely distributed to employees who already use microcomputers or to those who show the slightest inclination to use one. It could serve not only as a vehicle for communicating policy, but to describe microcomputer support services and to recruit new users.

The contents of a user's handbook might include

- Background on the company's current use of microcomputers
- Support services provided by a centralized microcomputer resource center
- Process for acquisition of a microcomputer system
- Information on current applications and uses
- Specific information on hardware and software
- Policies and procedures that affect users.

The format of a user's handbook is also critical. It should be brief, well written, and professional looking. The narrative should be directed at the microcomputer user exclusively in language appropriate to the average employee. The tone should be friendly and positive. (This may require some creative rewording, as many policies are very negative and censorial in tone.) Pictures, graphs, cartoons, and illustrations may be included to increase reader interest.

The idea is to design a booklet that readers will want to read from cover to cover. Keep in mind that this is not the definitive document on company microcomputer resources. It is a brief, printed booklet whose primary purpose is to engage the reader and convey some essential (but not necessarily all) company information about microcomputer use.

A sample *Microcomputer User's Handbook* is presented in Appendix D. Written for a mythical "SuperCorp," this sample suggests and illustrates the possible content and format for a booklet of this type.

Developing Corporate Microcomputer Support Services

16.1 JUSTIFYING MICROCOMPUTER SUPPORT SERVICES

A typical chronology of events for corporate microcomputer use goes something like this:

1. One or two corporate employees purchase and use a microcomputer. They obtain assistance in selecting hardware and software from a local vendor and (in most cases) from knowledgeable persons in the company data-processing department
2. Within a short time, other employees become interested and more hardware purchases are made.
3. These few users learn how to use their microcomputer from the vendor, from reading manuals, from each other, and from a lot of trial and error.
4. Over time, additional microcomputers are purchased (very likely different makes and models). The use is very exploratory, involving spreadsheet programs and graphics. Users expend a great deal of personal as well as company time developing their microcomputer skills.

5. General corporate interest is sparked, in part by heavy mass media advertising and by what is seen as wide corporate acceptance.

6. Other users get interested in microcomputers for specific applications that cannot be done with generic software. New special-purpose programs must be designed and written. Frequent demands are made on other users and the resident computer professionals for assistance.

7. New software programs are purchased frequently. Many are shelved after a short trial because they will not do easily what the purchaser thought they would do. They are difficult to operate, or they fail to work for lack of memory, graphics capability, or data incompatibilities. Software selection is more opportunistic than the result of systematic evaluation.

8. The manager of data processing voices complaints that microcomputer users are demanding too much time of the data-processing staff.

9. Microcomputer users voice complaints that their reliance on vendors for technical and other kinds of assistance is not wholly satisfactory.

10. More microcomputers are purchased.

11. Someone suggests the need for more organized corporate microcomputer support services.

Although this scenario may not be the same for all companies, it seems to bear a close resemblance to the early microcomputer experiences of many companies. It suggests a few *elementary truths* about microcomputer use in corporate settings.

One of those truths is that *microcomputers are not simple to use after all.* They *do* require someone around who understands the technical mysteries of computer hardware and software to lend assistance as the occasion arises. And those occasions do arise with great regularity.

A second elementary truth is that *individual users, acting on their own interests, are not concerned about issues of machine and data compatibility.* The problems of incompatibility have already been described.

Yet another truth is that *microcomputer users are not, and cannot be expected to be, experts in hardware and software selection.* They easily fall victim to flashy advertising claims. And while they should have a voice in selection, responsible and objective evaluation is a major undertaking.

These elementary truths add up to just one overriding truth: *microcomputer users cannot go it alone.* They need help—qualified technical, professional assistance so that their time is spent utilizing microcomputer technology for the benefit of the company, not trying to figure out how to make the technology work as it is supposed to work.

The issue for any company making major use of microcomputers is clear. Either the company provides support services to microcomputer users, or the company must limit microcomputer use to those who already have the necessary expertise. Anything less and the company will not reap the full benefits of microcomputer technology or will pay a high price for users to diddle with the technology on company time. The cost in lost production and simple employee frustration makes the last option a poor one indeed. A large number of companies have decided that some sort of centralized microcomputer support services are essential if the company is to realize the best return on its investment in microcomputers.

The costs for such services are similar to those for any technical support. Fortunately, it does not take an army to provide such services. Three to five professional staffers can support a rather significant number of microcomputer users.

Some may argue that a dedicated staff just to support microcomputer users makes the technology prohibitively expensive. Perhaps. But the trade-offs are not without their respective costs either. The real question is whether greater productivity is obtained by letting users go it alone or by providing them with professional guidance and support.

A growing number of companies opt for the latter. They see information technology as an essential part of modern corporate life and justify the costs to support this technology as simply the costs of doing business in a rapidly changing, highly technical, and information-intensive world.

16.2 USER NEEDS AND SUPPORT SERVICES

Once a company is committed to the idea of developing microcomputer support services, it must necessarily focus on the kinds of activities and resources that need to be provided.

Support services should be created to serve the needs of specific users. All microcomputer users will at some point be faced with:

- Deciding whether or not they should use a microcomputer for carrying out one or more of their job activities
- Deciding what microcomputer hardware is "right" for them
- Learning what a microcomputer does and how it can be operated
- Deciding which of several software programs to use
- Learning how to use specific programs
- Hooking up new equipment when it arrives
- Fixing equipment when it does not work right
- Trying out new software when it seems appropriate and useful to a job task
- Learning to use different computers and possibly learning to design and write their own programs

These are not necessarily all the needs of microcomputer users, but it is a fairly representative list. These needs may be identified with one of five service areas:

1. Microcomputer acquisition services
2. Hardware support services
3. Software support services
4. Technical assistance services
5. User training and support services

16.3 MICROCOMPUTER ACQUISITION SERVICES

Microcomputer hardware acquisition is typically the primary focus of microcomputer management, yet it is one area that is most often troublesome. The most frequently asked question by microcomputer newcomers is, What microcomputer should I buy? Unfortunately, that is the *wrong* first question.

Among the first questions that a potential microcomputer user *should* ask (or ought to be directed to ask) are: What can a microcomputer do for me?, What will it cost?, and Is it worth it?

The process of asking these questions and getting answers is the process of acquisition. Supporting the acquisition process ought to be a major function of a microcomputer resource center, because a bad decision made at this point (such as a poor match between the software and the job that is to be done, or a poor match between the user and the software, or a poor match between software and hardware) may spell the difference between success and failure for the user. It also may influence all future microcomputer uses.

What is *acquisition* exactly? It is a formal procedure for helping potential microcomputer users do three things: (1) to examine their job/task needs to see if they would actually benefit from microcomputerization, (2) to look at the utility of various microcomputer systems in terms of particular applications needed, and (3) to formalize the specifications for a system purchase. Step 2 is not done unless it is decided after doing step 1 that the job/task would benefit from microcomputerization, and step 3 is not done unless it is determined in step 2 that a particular system configuration would indeed suit the needs of the job and the user.

Every company that uses microcomputer technology in a significant way should have a formal microcomputer acquisition procedure. This procedure should be invoked with each department or individual requesting the purchase of a system. The procedure should not be to discourage or set up paper-work roadblocks; it should be a process that ensures that all the right questions are asked and answered appropriately. The process should be one that demonstrates that thought and judgment have been exercised in selecting hardware and software and, most importantly, that if they are purchased they will indeed do the job.

While such a procedure can become complex and time consuming, it need not be. However, any amount of time spent at this stage would seem trivial in comparison to the time that would be wasted if the wrong system is selected.

Three approaches might be taken to justify a microcomputer purchase. The first is a very brief procedure in which the potential user provides off-the-cuff answers to questions asked by, say, the manager of the microcomputer resource center. Though convenient, such a procedure offers little opportunity to scrutinize and validate the potential microcomputer application.

The second approach would require the user to fill out a carefully constructed questionnaire. The information given on this questionnaire could then be used as the basis for a more objective and considered evaluation of the appropriateness of microcomputer use and the proposed system.

A third approach is more elaborate. It is the same approach taken by large data-processing organizations in analyzing and justifying new system purchases. This procedure requires several days, weeks, or perhaps months of detailed study of the potential benefits and trade-offs.

Obviously, the first approach is less than adequate. The third approach is overkill. (More time and dollars could be spent in doing the third procedure than several microcomputer systems would cost.) The second approach is a reasonable compromise. The use of a constructed questionnaire, coupled with a separate review, provides a quick but focused appraisal of the planned microcomputer system.

A model questionnaire, the *Microcomputer Requirements Analysis and System Definition,* is included in Appendix E. This form asks very pointed questions that give outside reviewers a great deal of information useful in judging the legitimacy of the request. The questionnaire also forces the person making the request to consider his or her use of the microcomputer system and its benefits to the company. Employees who have no real justification for using a microcomputer generally withdraw their request voluntarily when they realize they have only nebulous or weak reasons for making the request in the first place.

The review of microcomputer purchase requests should be carried out by those who have a balanced perspective of microcomputer uses and company goals. It should also be done by persons who are in a position of judging fairly the information provided by the requester. Reviewers should examine the request with critical attention to the following:

- Does this employee have a real need?
- Would any microcomputer system resolve this need?
- Could an adequate resolution of this need be accomplished by a change in job procedures? By other existing technology or systems?
- If a software purchase is specified, is the software appropriate to both the job to be done and to this particular user?
- If a hardware purchase is specified, is the hardware configuration appropriate to the software selected and to this particular user?
- Does this system, as specified, allow for future expansion? Is expansion likely? How would such expansion affect this system?
- What specific benefits will accrue to the company if this system is approved for purchase and made operational?

- What are the direct and indirect costs?
- Do the proposed benefits justify the expected expenditures?
- Will acceptance or denial of the request cause the company any new problems?

The process of reviewing a purchase request should be done with serious intent and with the best interests of the company in mind. If microcomputer technology is generally a good thing for the company, then all requests that can reasonably be justified ought to be approved (subject to the availability of funds, of course).

The general attitude of the reviewers ought to be to assist employees to get a request approved. If reviewers feel that the proposed hardware configuration or software selection is less than optimal and want the person making the request to consider other alternatives, they should work collaboratively with the employee making the request to affect those changes.

16.4 USER TRAINING AND SUPPORT

Next to supporting users with the acquisition of microcomputers, the most important microcomputer support function is user training. Getting users equipped with hardware and software is, admittedly, very important, but the specific brands, models, and configurations of hardware and software will rapidly become standardized for the company. *The most continuously demanding effort placed on the microcomputer resource center will be for user training and support.* If the true needs of users are responded to, the majority of staff time will be expended in this effort.[1]

Training services may include:

- Demonstrations of hardware and software applications to individuals and small groups
- Introductory (get acquainted) classroom seminars on microcomputer applications
- Intensive (skill-building) workshops on specific software packages and programming
- Coordination of special seminars and training provided by outside consultants and vendors
- Individual and small-group tutorials on a wide range of microcomputer topics

Training may be conducted both formally or informally, consisting of classes, small groups, or individual tutorials. General user information can usually be communicated through brief, stand-up lectures and "chalk-and-talk" presentations, but

---

[1]This may be an important fact to consider when making staffing decisions.

the development of individual user skills will require hands-on involvement with microcomputer systems over a period of several hours.

The learning efficiency of users will depend on (1) their own aptitude and motivations for working with a computer, (2) their previous experience with similar systems, and (3) the quality of the training itself. Novices require from 4 to 15 hours of hands-on instruction to develop a sufficient level of skill on word-processing or spreadsheet programs. Some users may prefer to work independently and coach themselves from manuals, relying on trainers for only occasional assistance. Others will require extensive trainer support either in the classroom or in a one-on-one instructional setting. Users who show anxiety in using a microcomputer may require more frequent personal support over a longer period of time. Adults often learn most effectively in the presence of a friendly, patient, and supportive human being of similar age and experience.

General classroom presentations for large groups of employees on a voluntary basis should not be overlooked as an effective way to build microcomputer knowledge and a predisposition to use the technology. Experience has shown that, when such courses are made available to employees on a volunteer basis, they are usually well attended, and they can reduce the need for more time-intensive, hands-on instruction. Such courses can also be offered outside normal business hours.

There is also a natural inclination for microcomputer users to want to share their microcomputing experiences with other users. This inclination to share ought to be used to advantage. A great deal of learning can take place informally through employee-to-employee interaction. The microcomputer support center should stimulate and encourage such interaction whenever possible. Activities might include:

- A *user group* that meets periodically to share information about current projects, problems, and special applications
- A *newsletter* that is developed and supported by the user group
- A *bulletin board* of useful hints and user information (the bulletin board itself might be accessible through a network or by dial-up data communications)
- *Speakers* and special *seminars* along with other activities of interest to users

The corporate sponsorship of employee-run groups should be done with tact and finesse. User groups work best when they determine their own directions and when they are truly user led. The appropriate role of a microcomputer support center is to get things started and then back off and let the natural leaders take over. The appropriate involvement of a microcomputer resource center in user groups is to provide a place to meet, publicize meetings, and provide refreshments.

The training function cannot be overemphasized. Whether or not microcomputers live or die within a corporate environment depends critically on user knowledge and skills, and the only way that a company can affect an employee's knowledge and skills is through some form of training. The success of an entire microcomputer effort will ultimately depend on the successful development and management of user training.

In the final analysis, the most significant corporate microcomputer resource will not be the number and dollar amount of microcomputers acquired and housed within the company, but the increased capability of employees to use and to understand computer technology in general. The real payoff will come not when an individual can operate a specific program on a specific piece of equipment, but when most employees can comfortably and fluently move from computer system to computer system with little concern about operating technicalities and with equally effective results. Such *computer literacy* is a worthwhile goal and certainly within the purview of a microcomputer resource center organization.

16.5 HARDWARE-RELATED SUPPORT SERVICES

Microcomputer hardware is typically the most visible aspect of microcomputer support services. It is the hardware that commands initial attention. Because of its tangibility, hardware gives a sense of realness to the abstract concepts of microcomputing, the complexities of software programs, and new ways of processing and dealing with corporate information.

The hardware-related support services offered by a microcomputer resource center may include the following:

- Introducing users to various microcomputer hardware components
- Demonstrations of computers and peripheral equipment, such as printers, graphics plotters, and modems
- Recommendations of hardware for specific applications
- Information on brands and models, capacity and speed, functions, costs, delivery times, and so on
- Assistance in selecting appropriate equipment and writing purchase specifications
- Evaluating new hardware products

Except for the last item listed, these support services are dependent on the company not having identified a standard microcomputer hardware configuration. If and when a company adopts a hardware standard, these support services may all but disappear.

Companies that adopt a hardware standard do so to ensure that different systems when purchased will be compatible with each other. Given that a single microcomputer (or possibly two) can be used for all identified microcomputer applications, a company can feel at ease in the knowledge that any system can read the disk data files of any other system, that the operating systems are the same, making it possible to use the same software, that parts and components such as memory boards, plotters, and printers can be shared, and that users will not be faced with having to learn the operational complexities of several different systems.

There are also some good reasons for a company not settling on a standard too soon. Limiting the company to a single computer, which may not have all the required capabilities or functions (or worse, cannot be modified), may actually handicap efforts to get more widespread use of microcomputer technology. A standard that is set too high wastes dollars on capabilities that may never be needed or utilized by some users. A standard that is set too low soon requires that other (nonstandard) systems be purchased. The enforcement of a company standard should always be open to review, and there should be an exceptions procedure for purchasing the nonstandard system when the exception can be justified.

Selection of a hardware standard is not easy. The number of products on the market makes any comprehensive and objective evaluation of every competing system too costly and time consuming to be practical. Nevertheless, someone has to make the choice. Some companies purchase several different microcomputer makes and models and evaluate their use over an extended period of time. Others rely on the reputation of the vendor or the manufacturer, and perhaps all are influenced by published critical reviews and advertising.

Whatever the method for selecting hardware, some guidelines should be followed. These guidelines serve as a starting point:

1. *Select hardware that has a large base of vendor support.* The reason should be obvious. More vendors selling a given product probably means that the product has somewhat proved itself in the market. It may not be the best buy, but it certainly is not a bad buy.

2. *Select hardware that allows the use of interchangeable circuit boards.* Without this capability, there is no opportunity for increasing the functional capacity of the hardware beyond its original configuration. Expansion, up-grading, and enhancement of performance are impossible.

3. *Select hardware that uses standard input and output devices.* Keyboards should have a standard typewriter keyboard layout, number-key pads, cursor-control keys, and function keys. Monitor screens should display a standard 25 lines of 80 characters per line.[2] Printers should use the same communications protocols so that different printers can be shared or interchanged without difficulty. And, although not critical, it is convenient if hardware utilizes the same types of cabling and connectors.

4. *Select hardware with the assumption that it will be upgraded and enhanced once and perhaps several times over the life of the product.* Choose hardware that manufacturers other than the original manufacturer support. This sets the stage for de facto standards and keeps prices down through competition.

---

[2]There are exceptions. Some graphics cards permit displays of up to 120 characters. These expanded graphics capabilities are especially useful in working with spreadsheets and accounting reports. The essential point is that nonstandard input and output should be *in addition to, not in place of,* generally acceptable industry standards.

5. *Select hardware with the assumption that it will eventually be interconnected in a communications network.* Even though current applications only require stand-alone microcomputers, it is inevitable that microcomputers will assume the role of workstations for corporate data and voice communications networks. Microcomputers that do not readily lend themselves to networking will unquestionably become obsolete long before those that do.

Even with the best guidelines, it is likely that mistakes will be made in selecting hardware. There may be some consolation in the knowledge that the perfect microcomputer has not been made and never will be made. All designs are a compromise of function and cost, and all are experimental in the sense that they have been developed for an entirely new group of users about which little is yet known. At this time, the ideal microcomputer is one that meets a company's needs over the next few years.

16.6 SOFTWARE-RELATED SUPPORT SERVICES

The selection of appropriate applications software will represent one of the single most difficult problems for most users. Assistance provided by the microcomputer resource center staff to new users will be of paramount importance. Regardless of how sophisticated or user friendly the microcomputer hardware or how effectively the training is carried out, if the application software is not appropriate to the work task, the use of the microcomputer will be a failure. *Selection of software is the single most important decision in the acquisition of a microcomputer system.*

Software-related services provided by the microcomputer support center may include:

- Demonstrations of various software programs
- Recommendations of specific software packages for particular job applications
- Assistance in determining the availability of specially needed software
- Information on software costs, data formats and compatibility, licensing restrictions, and whether or not a particular software product is copyable and usable in hard-disk systems
- Assistance in getting started with a particular software package, and configuring the drives, screens, and printers.

In addition to services delivered directly to users, the microcomputer resource center may indirectly support users by:

- Reviewing and evaluating new software products
- Working for the adoption of company-standard software

- Establishing and maintaining a company software library of public-domain, noncopyrighted, employee-contributed, and company employee developed programs and routines
- Establishing and maintaining a documents library of technical information, user's manuals, and reference literature

Not all software programs, even for the same function, are appropriate for all users. A given program may have more features and capabilities, but it may be less appropriate for the new user than a simpler, easier-to-operate program. A secretary will undoubtedly want a full-featured word-processing program even though it may be difficult to learn to use. That same word-processing program might not be acceptable to the person who only drafts a memo now and then. A simple, menu-oriented word-processing program would be more sensible. Software should be matched not only to the user function, but to the user's own level of competence and aptitude. Even though it may seem wasteful to purchase three or four different spreadsheet or word-processing packages, this investment toward finding the most productive software will be repaid many times over.

It is very important for a company to evaluate software packages within the company itself. On-site, hands-on operation is really the only way to detect the idiosyncracies and shortcomings of a software package. This sort of testing is absolutely necessary when selecting major applications packages such as database management systems, integrated spreadsheet and graphics programs, and word-processing software.

Vendors cannot be relied on to recommend the best software. There are too many "situation variables" for their recommendations to be meaningful. Also, vendors usually stock a limited line of software, and their choices are usually influenced more by profit margin than firsthand knowledge about a software product's utility in a given work setting.

Software reviews appearing in microcomputer magazines are useful in pointing out different features of programs, but, again, they cannot be relied on as the only source of evaluation. Magazine publishers are understandably loath to offend potential software product advertisers, but the quality of published reviews is steadily improving. Publishers are becoming more willing to identify poor software that is on the market and to indicate particular weaknesses in particular programs. Their reviews best serve as a starting point to limit the number of software packages that may need to be evaluated in-house. Reviews that apply the same evaluative criteria to a number of software programs are especially useful. Companies can then start their own evaluation with the knowledge that they are evaluating the best on the market.

Current users of microcomputer software are usually a good source of information about software, although even here some skepticism is in order. Users may have had experience with only one software product and therefore may have little base for comparison. Also, users are often very loyal to a particular product simply because they have learned to adapt to its peculiarities and compensate for its short-comings.

Whatever and however software is selected, it is vital that the microcomputer resource center staff become very familiar (if not reasonably competent) with all software packages in general use in the company. They should know, at a minimum, how to initiate the program, how to make backups, how to call up the menus, and how to initiate program commands. They should also have a good understanding about which programs may work best for a particular application and for particular types of users. It is also imperative that they have a full working knowledge of the operating systems currently in use in the company.

Even though software will be selected to meet specific user needs, some preliminary selection guidelines may prove useful. Appendix F provides a series of questions that may be helpful.

Finally, as part of software support to users, it is especially important for a microcomputer resource center to maintain a documents library. This may never amount to more than a shelf containing a copy of all hardware and software documents (manuals, user guides, and technical manuals) that are used by the company, but it may prove to be the single most valuable microcomputer resource. Technical problems frequently require referring back to the manual, and the time to respond to a technical problem is usually a function of how long it takes to locate the appropriate reference manual.

Such a reference library should have a policy that does not permit reference documents to be removed from the library. The reasons are obvious but are often overlooked when the equipment is purchased by widely separated departments. It may also be appropriate to keep several copies of frequently used manuals that can be loaned out as users request them.

16.7 REPAIR AND MAINTENANCE

The repair and maintenance of microcomputer equipment does not have to be a major effort for most microcomputer resource centers. Microcomputer equipment is highly reliable, and the failure rate after the first 30 days or so (while the equipment is still under warranty) is extremely low.

This does not mean that there should be no repair and maintenance services. This should be one of the services provided by the microcomputer resource center. But these activities will focus mostly on initial hardware hook-ups and periodic maintenance and will exist more for the sake of convenience than from necessity.

Technical services may include the following:

- Unpacking, hook-up, and check-out of new equipment
- Installing new equipment in its permanent location
- Making up special cables for printers and modems

- Installing memory and graphics boards
- Troubleshooting
- Minor repairs
- Periodic maintenance
- Coordination with outside repair facilities
- Administrative work connected with service contracts
- Making arrangements for loaner equipment when the need is critical

Microcomputers have very few technician-serviceable parts, and in most cases no attempt should be made to repair the circuit boards themselves. The usual approach taken in servicing microcomputer equipment is the *swap-out* approach, which refers to the practice of removing a suspected circuit board and replacing it with another known to be functional until the faulty circuit board is found. The faulty board is then shipped back to the manufacturer for repair or replacement.

It is a good practice to establish with vendors at the time of purchase how repairs will be handled under warranty and after warranties expire. Service contracts are available for both on-site and carry-in service for a specific period. If service contracts are part of the original purchase, the effective date should begin on the date the warranties expire, not on the date of the purchase itself, since there is no benefit in doubling up on service protection during the warranty period.

A company should carefully study its own need for service contracts on microcomputer equipment. Because microcomputer equipment is highly reliable, the actual cost of infrequent repair may be far less than the ongoing cost of service contracts. The dollars saved may be better spent in providing a few backup or loaner systems. Unlike mainframe computer equipment, downtime on a microcomputer is usually not so critical. If a microcomputer application is critical, it will be necessary to arrange for the temporary use of a loaner until the problem is fixed anyway.

No expensive test equipment is required for the technical service function, but a simple set of tools and maintenance supplies are handy. A fairly complete tool kit would include screwdrivers, nut drivers, needle-nosed and regular pliers, a soldering iron (for making up cables), a VOM (volt/ohm meter for checking continuity), and supplies such as electrical tape, nylon cable ties, solder (rosin cored), spray-on glass cleaner (for cleaning monitor screens and cabinets), antistatic spray, and floppy disk cleaning kits.

16.8 A SUPPORT SERVICES PHILOSOPHY

The obvious way to deliver corporate microcomputer support is through a *centralized microcomputer support service center*. The term "microcomputer resource center" has been used throughout this chapter. This term is used by several companies as it projects an appropriate image for the kinds of support services offered to microcomputer users.

A name that has been adopted by some companies is Microcomputer Store. This appellation has caught on with a few companies and it will likely be heard for awhile, although its use is somewhat unfortunate because it tends to place too much emphasis on "things"—that is, the hardware and software. A *store* is a place where one buys something, and while selling potential users may be the main emphasis of some corporate microcomputer organizations, the long-term effect is that too much attention is focused on technical gadgetry.

A better image for a microcomputer support "center" is one that projects the seriousness of business information technology. It should provide a friendly atmosphere, to be sure, but it should just as importantly be a place to talk with knowledgeable people about day-to-day business problems and possible technological solutions to those problems. It could be a place where potential users have the opportunity to actually try out microcomputer hardware and software on a specific work-related task, but the emphasis should be on people, their work, their work problems, and ways of using technology to solve those problems. *The primary emphasis, most definitely, should not be on hardware.*

Names like Microcomputer Support Center or Microcomputer Resource Center seem to be more in keeping with the real mission of this organizational unit. Although any name that emphasizes the support and service philosophy should work just fine.

What is significant here is the philosophy and tone adopted by the manager and staff of a microcomputer resource center. If the philosophy is to control users, if the association between users and microcomputer resource center staff is primarily a negative one, or if the purpose is merely to impress with technical wizardry, the success of a microcomputer resource center is doubtful. However, if the focus is on corporate problems and productivity and if the philosophy is to serve users by responding to their requests with an enthusiastic yes and an honest attempt to follow through in providing assistance, success can almost be guaranteed.

CHAPTER

17

Planning for the Future: Microcomputers and Megatrends

Microcomputers, for all their newness, are nearly a decade old. Their invention, use, sudden popularity, and widespread acceptance by both corporate users and private individuals has all taken place since the mid-1970s. Much has taken place in that span of time. The first five years were largely dominated by concerns about hardware. Users were technically oriented and many were already computer professionals. During the second five years, concerns shifted toward software and enhanced system performance, in part brought about by the sudden popularity and widespread acceptance by noncomputer trained business professional users.

The next several years should see yet another shift of attention, but not necessarily away from hardware and software (their development will continue almost indefinitely). Attention will increasingly focus on the user/microcomputer relationship and how microcomputers can be assimilated into our everyday work and leisure lives.

Microcomputers (or some form of microcomputer-derived technology) will most surely play an increasingly important role in *how* work is done in corporate settings. It is appropriate to direct our attention in this final chapter to the future of microcomputing and anticipate its developing role and impact.

17.1 WILL MICROCOMPUTER TECHNOLOGY PREVAIL?

A relevant question posed by corporate managers thinking about microcomputers is, Will the microcomputer prevail? Will it be microcomputer technology that succeeds in resolving at least part of the corporate information dilemma? Can microcomputers really tackle industrial-strength corporate information problems? Will microcomputers really pay for themselves over the long haul? Are there any guarantees that a major investment in microcomputer technology will be a sound business investment?

The simple, unadulterated truth is that no one knows the answers to these questions. Only time and experience are going to vindicate our best guesses. But there are a lot of signs that suggest that it will be microcomputers that will actually carry us into the information age.

Certainly, some form of user-oriented, information processing technology is inevitable. The conditions that stimulated the microcomputer revolution in the first place—advances in computer technology, rapidly changing and demanding business information needs, favorable costs of the technology, and the eager acceptance of microcomputers by companies and individuals alike—are not abating.

In fact, predictions are that sometime in the foreseeable future the following points may be realized:

- The volume (explosion) of technical and business information will continue at an increasing rate indefinitely.
- Companies themselves will generate more data and information, which in turn will need to be processed and acted on more quickly.
- The ratio of white-collar to blue-collar jobs will increase to handle the increased information load.
- Business efficiencies will be tightly linked to data- and information-processing (both human and automated) efficiencies.

Some companies are already operating in an information-crisis mode where there are information overloads and data-processing bottlenecks. More companies are going to be joining their ranks unless they act soon.

The upshot is this: business runs on information. Information is the life's blood of all modern corporate organizations, and without the appropriate information available to managers, employees, and customers in the most timely fashion, very little business can get done. Consequently efficient data and information processing are essential, and microcomputers and other end-user-oriented mainframe computer systems must be at least part of the solution. There are no alternatives.

17.2 WHAT IS AHEAD FOR CORPORATE MICROCOMPUTER USERS?

Assuming the inevitability of microcomputer use in our companies into the foreseeable future, what can we expect in the way of development and improvements? What is ahead for corporate microcomputer users?

The whole brief history of microcomputing has been characterized by change and improvement, and there is no indication of a slowdown. In short, the future of microcomputing is going to be like its past, only more so. Over the next several years we are likely to see a rapid expansion of the use of microcomputers in a variety of configurations for a wide variety of applications. The hardware will get better, the software will get smarter, the users will get more productive.

There is no promise of any radical new developments, but the industry has never failed to provide surprises. More than likely the next decade will be spent in standardizing, improving, and refining the basic hardware and software that already exists.

17.3 HARDWARE TRENDS

What hardware innovations *are* we likely to see over the next few years? Mostly improvements on existing technology with a few notable exceptions.

In the past, we have seen increases in computer processor speed and a decrease in component size. The race goes on, but it cannot continue indefinitely. Some microprocessors already have far more processing power than a single user can use. The trend is less apt to be a new super microchip than a composite architecture that uses *multiple cooperating microprocessors* to achieve overall increased performance and output. New chips usually demand new operating systems, and a generation of independent users who have struggled to learn one operating system are going to resist having to learn yet another.

Multitasking operations along with multiuser microcomputer systems may increase the demand for microcomputers with increased processing capacity. But single-user, stand-alone microcomputers tied into a network may prove a more economical and workable arrangement.

Two areas that may demand substantially more processing power than most microcomputers can now provide are graphics and voice input. But even these systems could be designed to tie into existing microcomputer systems.

The size of microcomputers will not change a great deal either. Battery-operated portables are likely, but the nature of microcomputer input and output devices places real limitations on microcomputer size. Keyboards can only be reduced so much before they are too small to be used efficiently by average adult-sized hands.

Likewise, video display screens of less than about 7 inches become very difficult to use for even moderate periods of use. It seems reasonable that flat-screen technology would be a definite advantage for microcomputer displays both to reduce the size and power requirements for portable computers and to improve the positioning of the screen for everyday use. (Flat screens could be hung inconspicuously on an office wall or designed in pop-up desk-top instruments.)

The use of other input and output devices may offer some new surprises, but it is not likely that even existing devices will survive over the next decade. The mouse is inherently limited by the need to remove one's hands from a keyboard and by the requirement of a clear desk space to roll it around. It also requires a clumsy cord attachment and is yet another implement with which the user has to contend.

Touch-screen technology offers more convenience since the user points directly to areas on the screen without having to look elsewhere. Unfortunately, touch-screen techniques still require users to remove at least one hand from the keyboard. The touch-screen also has a fairly coarse resolution, being limited to the size of the human finger.

A light pen, while offering higher point resolution than a touch screen, is encumbered like the mouse with a connecting cord. A wireless light pen would overcome this problem, but it still would require removal of a hand from the keyboard.

Digitizer tablets, joy sticks, track balls, and the foot-operated mouse, while useful for certain applications, all have similar limitations and disadvantages. Better input devices will likely be created that permit rapid and accurate cursor control from the keyboard itself.

Graphics may be one area where hardware will improve dramatically. Most currently available microcomputer systems only produce images of limited resolution. New techniques will integrate graphics and video information to produce images of much greater resolution and quality. Users already have expectations of images at least as good as those produced by their home television sets. They are not going to settle for long for anything inferior to that standard.

The ideal display screen would present ultrahigh image resolution with unlimited colors and would permit the display of any size of page or presentation format. The current state of graphics technology is such that this ideal display is possible; however, images of this quality make very high demands on processing speed and memory. The economics of computer graphics technology may make it necessary for users to use existing graphics capabilities for some time.

Microcomputer applications involving data communications of every form—microcomputer-to-microcomputer and microcomputer-to-mainframe through both direct cable connections and telephone dial-up connections—are rapidly increasing, and such linkages will likely become the rule rather than the exception over the next few years.

But the additional cost of installing network communications circuit boards and the disappointing performance of early local area networking systems is tending to impede their widespread use within corporate settings. New digital communications systems that allow virtually any microcomputer system to interconnect with any other computer system at only a modest cost should stimulate widespread microcomputer-based networking.

Low cost microcomputer systems that integrate both voice and data communications will substantially boost microcomputer networking because the costs of separate voice- and data-processing services and instruments can be compressed into a single service and instrument. Ultimately, the costs for integrated data and voice communications systems should be cheaper than the sum of costs for separate and individual systems.

Changes in mass data storage will come about through the development of still cheaper and higher-capacity data storage devices. Optical systems offer the highest storage densities, but there are substantial technical obstacles to overcome before optical storage and retrieval systems are available at a price suitable for microcomputer users. Optical systems will undoubtedly be used where high data volumes are needed by many users, but for the next few years magnetic media will continue to be widely used. Magnetic media technology is well understood, and improvements and storage densities are continually increasing, while costs to the consumer are steadily decreasing.

Conversational-level voice input and output are among the most exciting computer capabilities we can imagine, but voice input is still years away from becoming a practical reality. The difficulties of analyzing conversational voice input and processing it for any meaningful use are enormous. State-of-the-art voice analysis is primitive even for extremely powerful mainframe computers.

It is possible that we will see increasing use of voice input for rather specialized microcomputer-based applications such as process control, robotics, and real-time data entry, but such voice input systems use a limited vocabulary and all require some level of special knowledge and expertise on the part of the user.

While hardware technology has played the most important role in shaping microcomputer use in the past, it cannot continue to have such a dominant role. This does not mean that new technical improvements will not be forthcoming. Certainly, they will, and they will make life easier and more productive for the user. It just means that software developments and the users themselves must now catch up to the capabilities of the technology.

17.4 SOFTWARE TRENDS

Software will always play an important role because it is software that bridges the capabilities of the hardware with the needs and the applications of the users. There is no question that microcomputer software has gone through several periods of refinement over the past few years, and two trends seem to have dominated microcomputer software development. The first trend has been to make microcomputer software easier to use, more user friendly. The other trend has been to integrate separate-function generic programs like spreadsheets, database management, and graphics into a single integrated program. It is highly likely that both trends will continue for some time.

The trend toward easier-to-use software is a result of direct influence from the marketplace. More and more microcomputer purchases are made by nontechnical users. It is natural that software designers would want to design software for these users. Most software advertisements include the phrase easy-to-use and it is clear that they are pitching their products toward nontechnical consumers. *Easier-to-use* does not necessarily mean *easy* to use. But software designs may one day achieve that status.

The most obvious design technique is the use of menus. Menus present the user with several choices of activities and then prompt for the next action. The menu approach is extremely useful in that it relieves the user from having to remember a list of commands and the appropriate syntax. The biggest disadvantage to menu programs is that they tend to be somewhat slow and cumbersome. A user who already knows and uses commands skillfully can usually work with a given program far faster.

Recently a number of programs have been designed with one or more menus appearing on-screen simultaneously through a programming technique known as *windowing*. The press of a few keys or the use of a mouse makes a series of individual menus or sub-menus appear on the screen. The availability of these "pop-up" or "pull-down" menus readily at hand is a real convenience to users.

The overall effect of several menus displayed at once is very geometric and on a color screen is very colorful. But there are drawbacks. Apart from the convenience offered by these menus, the multiple overlays simultaneously displayed often presents little more that a confusing, visual clutter. From a serious user's standpoint, the simultaneous display of so much information is a distraction. Rather than simplify the life of the user, such software designs may tend to complicate it.

The use of windows and other graphics techniques is generally a good trend, but some programs seem to use graphics for graphics sake, and not because they provide real benefits to the user. There is a significant difference between good screen design and mere technical pyrotechnics.

Other useful features are context-sensitive on-screen help messages available at the touch of a key, appropriately programmed and labeled function keys, and the "un-do" key which allows a user to back out of a selected choice and return to an earlier screen.

The intention of all user-friendly design techniques, presumably, is to assist the user. Some work and some do not. The best designs are those that are sensitive to users' needs and expectations. These programs seem to understand what a user may be feeling at a given time and provide frequent messages and reassurances that "all is well." New users (and a few experienced ones) have a lot of anxiety. A simple message displayed at an appropriate time can eliminate that anxiety. A message that tells the user that a particular activity is in progress (as when the computer is sorting or making long calculations) is a trivial programming task and relieves the user from having to worry about what is currently happening.

Some program designers are content with making a program only functionally complete. They do not fully comprehend that most microcomputing is an interactive process between human beings and machines and that they, as the persona within the machine, must *communicate* with the user.

While there is considerable room for improvement in the design of microcomputer software, good design is becoming more the rule than the exception. Some of the best software that exists (including software for mainframe computers) has been designed for microcomputers. Some microcomputer software is truly a paragon of computer program design.

A second major software trend is program integration. Integration is simply the practice of designing and packaging various applications into a single software package. Integrated programs often include most or all the generic applications (word processing, spreadsheet, graphics, database management, and data communications).

Two methods are used to integrate what have typically been separate program functions. One method combines several applications into a single program by design. As the software is developed, all these functions are programmed into that one program package and are purchased as a single unit. A second method is a program that simply allows the user to combine existing programs into what appears to the user to be an integrated set of programs. The integration program serves as a kind of master menu that lets the user quickly move back and forth between different independent application programs. These programs also assist in transferring data between programs and in managing which of several programs is resident in memory at any given time.

The first method of integration has been a huge commercial success. The advantages to the user in integrating several applications without having to be concerned with data compatibility and bother with data conversions and without having to learn to use several different programs are obvious.

The second method, while a relative newcomer on the integration scene, promises to be even more useful. Such programs make it possible for users who are already satisfied with their individual (nonintegrated) software packages to continue using that same software. They also make it possible to integrate other programs at a later time.

Integration is an approach to making life easier for the microcomputer user by making functional differences and operations transparent to the user. It is a concept that should become indigenous to all software design.

A more subtle trend in software design has been the gradual convergence of commands. Early software designers seemed determined to invent all new terms for common operations. The simple act of listing files from a disk directory might require the user to learn the terms *dir, directory, files, catalog,* and *cat* and then to remember which term was appropriate for a given system. The removal of a file from a disk could similarly employ one (or more) of these terms: *scratch, erase, kill, purge,* or *delete*. Every programmer could probably build a case why his or her word choice was more appropriate, but, in truth, any one of those terms is as good as another. Nothing is gained by insisting on uniquely worded commands for common operations. Consistency and the need to simplify what is already complicated should count for something.

Even within various versions of programming languages, BASIC, for example, the same keywords may invoke quite different processes. The more recent database management system languages generally tend to use similar command keywords, but there are usually just enough differences to force the user to refer back to the manual again and again to check commands and their syntax.

Users can only hope for the eventual development of a generic command language for operating systems and for database management systems languages that provide a standard set of commands. The development of a *common user interface language* (CUIL?) ought to be a high priority of software developers who could then tout their products as "easy to learn" on the basis that users already know how to operate their programs since they already know the common user interface language. A further benefit is that most user manuals could be reduced to a fraction of their present size, since a new set of commands would not have to be documented and taught to every new software purchaser.

A language composed of a common set of keywords and a universal syntax with the facility for hierarchical elaboration and command modification should allow the development of a command language that could quickly be learned and used by novices, yet offer unlimited sophistication and precise command notation for more experienced users. Such a language could be elegant in its simplicity, yet powerful in its execution. Is such a language too much to hope for? Hopefully not.

There is great excitement about the development of artificial intelligence (AI) techniques. These techniques promise to produce a computer revolution of their own, but at this time they are not used except in the most elementary way. It is reasonable to think that new software designs resulting from developments in AI will have an impact on how we approach and solve problems using the computer, and that these will be incorporated into microcomputer software. But many, many problems remain to be solved.

Much of human brainpower results from our ability to perceive large amounts of information as patterns and to process the patterns meaningfully. A human being, for example, can recognize one particular face in a crowd of several thousand faces and can do so almost instantly with a reliability approaching absolute certainty. A computer approaching the same task, if it could do it at all, might take hours or days of computer processing time, and the results would be very unreliable. Pattern recognition is not something a computer can do easily; and in comparison to human performance it is horrendously poor because computers, at least by current technological standards, must work (albeit quickly) with only a single data point at a time. This is an unfortunate stumbling block for artificial intelligence, because as human information and data-processing techniques go, pattern recognition and processing appear to be among the most powerful. AI programs currently achieve their results through a brute-force approach using very large, high-speed computers with mammoth memory capabilities. These techniques have almost no chance of being transported to microcomputers in the near future, if ever. Unless a breakthrough occurs, it is not likely that AI will make any significant impact on microcomputer software design for a number of years to come.

17.5 USER TRENDS

A functioning microcomputer system is made up of three essential components: hardware, software, and the user. Without all three, the system cannot function. The weakest of the three determines the upper bounds of system performance. If hardware components are pushed to their capacity by both the software and skilled users, then hardware becomes the limiting factor. (Over the short course of microcomputer history, the hardware has been the least limiting factor.) Few microcomputers have been pushed to their limits except in exceptional circumstances by highly skilled professionals and hobbyists. For most microcomputer users, however, the hardware and the best software offer more capability than users can successfully harness.

The role of the user in determining system performance cannot be overstated. It is the *user*, this third essential component, that will demand more attention in the future.

A tremendous limiting factor is the technical sophistication required of users. New users with no previous computer experience have to understand something about how a computer works in general, they must master a whole new technical jargon (if for no other purpose than to understand the user's manuals), they must learn the often abstruse and cryptic commands of the operating system, and they must develop skill in using the specific commands of whatever software packages they want to work with. In addition, a great many have to struggle with learning keyboard skills. Still others must spend time learning BASIC or some other programming language.

Although well trained in their own professional fields, users have to struggle with learning to think and organize their activities according to the structural dictates of spreadsheets, word processors, and other software programs.

In general, over the next decade the technology will continue to get easier to use. The operations of one microcomputer will be standardized to be very much like the operations of any other microcomputer. Learning how to use one system will be tantamount to learning how to use all of them. Technical knowledge and technical demands on users will be reduced to a minimum.

Even as the hardware becomes increasingly complex, the technical know-how required of users will get less demanding. Software programs will become increasingly sophisticated, but that sophistication will favor the nontechnical user. In a sense, microcomputer technology will leave the "stick shift" age and enter the "automatic shift" age of microcomputers. No longer will users have to understand "how it works," but only that for a given application it will get the user from here to there.

At the same time, users themselves will get smarter. They will know how to adapt their modes of thinking to better operate and work within the inherent limitations of the technology. And, most importantly, they will achieve not just a working knowledge about computers, but about information as well. The goal will shift from the need to become computer literate to allowing users to spend more time in developing their own information systems literacy.

One of the observations that can be made about the first decade of microcomputer use is that users were dominated by the technology. Hopefully, an observation that we will be able to make by the end of the second decade is that users are at least equal to its capabilities.

17.6 THE WORKSTATION CONCEPT

The fantasy of an electronic desk-top device that would provide communications, data retrieval, and clerical assistance is as old as science fiction itself. The utilitarian nature of the microcomputer is bringing us closer to the realization of that fantasy.

The term *workstation* is already used by several computer companies to describe a mainframe computer terminal or microcomputer that is capable of supporting several applications relevant to a particular job. The jobs supported, of course, are those that involve working with information—creating it, processing it, or communicating it to another user. The applications supported include word processing, calendars and scheduling, and usually some form of data communications and electronic mail.

Although the applications supported are highly useful, workstations in the future will be much more comprehensive in their ability to process and communicate data than present versions. They will be capable of handling virtually *all* data and information transactions. In addition to all generic applications, they will provide access to and means for highly specialized computing and data processing. They will also take on the existing functions of:

- Typewriters
- Calculators
- File cabinets and other data-storage devices
- Telephones
- Facsimile machines
- Copiers

- Calendars and schedule books
- Note pads
- Sketch and doodle pads (for full-color, three-dimensional, animated drawings)
- Phone directories, catalogs, dictionaries, and all variety of reference books and manuals
- Newspapers, magazines, and, in particular, technical journals
- Dictating machines

In addition, a full-function workstation in the future will be able to receive a whole spectrum of commercial television programs and video services. Users will be able to capture, store, and retrieve very high resolution still pictures as well as full color and motion video segments.

A full-function workstation will easily connect into local company networks, commercial dial-up databases and computer services, and it will link users around the world with each other by communications satellite.

The comprehensive electronic workstation will enable every homeowner to remotely monitor and control all types of mechanical and electronic devices, including heating systems, appliances, and security systems, through their home-based microcomputer workstation. These same workstations will also provide access 24 hours a day to a wide variety of educational and entertainment services.

When will such a workstation become a reality? Probably within the decade. From a purely technical standpoint, it could happen now. All the technologies necessary to produce such a workstation currently exist. Technical development is largely a matter of integrating the several separate and already existing technologies.

But the comprehensive workstation will likely become a reality only when it meets these criteria: (1) when the technologies are combined and marketed as a standard workstation unit, (2) when a single-unit workstation can provide services that are as reliable and convenient to use as separate technologies, and (3) when such workstations can be afforded by the average homeowner.

This last criterion is especially important. The workstation is potentially most useful *when it links users beyond the boundaries of a single company.* If the workstation is limited by cost to only a few users, its potential value, its growth, and its use will be severely retarded. One only has to look at the microcomputer market to see that the availability of low-cost microcomputers has contributed substantially to the success of microcomputers in general. The expensive, higher-priced microcomputer systems have not enjoyed the volume of sales nor the popularity of less expensive systems simply because they were out of the price range of the noncorporate buyer.

This does not mean that the lowest-priced systems will dominate the market. Quite the contrary. The lowest-priced microcomputers are naturally very limited in what they can do, and most users want real computer capabilities, not just toys. Buyers have already swung away from these low-priced toys to medium-priced systems, but it is doubtful if many individuals will invest in high-priced systems for their own private use. While companies will from time to time purchase the higher-priced systems (especially when those systems offer capabilities needed and available only in the higher-priced machines), the tendency will continue to be that company employees prefer to work with the same hardware and software at the office as they do at home.

It has been estimated that by the end of this century a full 75 to 90 percent of all corporate employees in white-collar jobs will use some sort of workstationlike device. While it may be difficult to envision a full 75 to 90 percent of all corporate employees working extensively with microcomputers, it is not difficult to see that, if mail is delivered electronically, and voice communications are part of the computer network, then virtually all managers and a very large percentage of those who spend most of their working day at a desk are going to have to require access to a workstation of some kind.

It is not possible to say at this moment whether it will be mainframe systems or microcomputer systems that evolve into fully integrated workstations. Centralized mainframe computer systems serving large numbers of corporate users through terminals are certainly one candidate, but placing a high value on independent, individual, and decentralized data processing makes microcomputers a logical candidate, too. Both mainframe systems and microcomputer systems appear to be developing in similar directions that place computer and data-processing capabilities into the hands of more corporate users.

Only time will determine whether large, centralized systems or small, decentralized microcomputer-based networks will serve best. Very likely the ultimate system will be a hybrid system utilizing the best both have to offer with neither technology dominating the other. There can be no doubt, however, that as society in general and business in particular move deeper into the information age microcomputers will play a major role—a role that is destined to get bigger and more important as time goes on.

In a society interconnected by workstations no longer would you hear the lament "If only we were in my office . . . " because it will be a simple matter for individuals to dial into their own personal workstation from any other workstation to obtain any information stored there. Access will be as convenient as the nearest telephone, and it is likely that public access workstations will be located everywhere—in homes, shopping centers, airports, and quite possibly in airplanes and personal automobiles. Electronic workstations will provide a global information and communications link similar to that provided by our worldwide telephone system, but with significantly greater information-processing and communications capabilities.

The capabilities of a comprehensive electronic workstation such as that just described are beyond the capabilities of microcomputers presently on the market, but that fact ought not to deter any company from moving ahead quickly with the fullest possible implementation of microcomputers. Today's microcomputers as we currently know and use them will provide the transition between fully separate information technologies (i.e., separate typewriters, copiers, telephones, computers, etc.) and fully integrated information-handling technologies.

A comprehensive electronic workstation on every employee's desk is not a certainty (nor perhaps desirable), but it is a fairly safe assumption that most corporate employees will use something very close to the kind of workstation described within five to ten years, a short time as corporate planning goes. Certainly, such important information-handling capabilities and the opportunities afforded business by microcomputers cannot be ignored.

17.7 THE BOTTOM LINE

The reader must have guessed by now that the central message of this book is that microcomputers are a vitally important technological resource for modern business. The bottom line is that they are here to stay—in their present configuration for a time, then evolving into a fully integrated computer/communications/information/thought-processing workstation over the next decade. They will serve as a better instrument for capturing, storing, retrieving, processing, and communicating information, better than any we have ever known. They will also serve as an instrument of change, as to how we think about data and information, how we work with it, and how we use it on a daily basis.

But an equally important message is that microcomputer technology must be managed wisely. Managers and all who influence the use of microcomputers within corporate settings need to recognize and deal with both the potential of the microcomputer and its limitations. They need to manage pro-actively, purposefully, and with the expectation that microcomputers, like other office technologies, can and should economically justify their own existence.

The issues surrounding which hardware and software to buy are critical issues, of this there can be no doubt. But an issue for companies as important as the technology itself is the impact that new information-handling modes will have on employees and company operations. Some job descriptions will change. Others will vanish or be consolidated into new job responsibilities. Procedures will be streamlined. Jobs may become more diversified.

No longer will job responsibilities necessarily need to be limited or partitioned on the basis of geographical location or proximity to other workers. Monitoring the status of operations will be as simple as punching in the right combination of keys on the most convenient workstation. Issues of security, privacy, and "big brother" will arise again and again. Changes will be frequent; and because every change extracts its toll of time, resources, and human stress, the sooner companies anticipate these changes and begin to deal with them, the smoother and less costly those changes will be for the company as a whole.

Will the workstation and/or the extensive use of microcomputers change the nature of human interaction? Without a doubt. As jobs change and normal patterns of socialization are interrupted, new patterns of interaction will have to be created. If the copy machine is displaced by information sent digitally over the computing network, then those who use their time at the copy machine for social chit-chat will no longer have that opportunity. New opportunities for direct contact socialization will have to be found.

Meetings called for the purpose of sharing data and information can be held via workstation conferences. But electronic meetings with low-quality voice and visual data transmission are likely to be avoided by most users. Interpersonal behavior is determined to a large degree by the nonverbal signals we send through voice inflection and body gestures. Any technology that interferes with this exchange of interpersonal information will be less useful than one that reproduces it with fidelity.

The widespread use of workstations, if they isolate or reduce interpersonal interaction, will probably require that enhanced opportunities for social contact be created. Workstation networks, like the telephone network, should also be used as a medium for increased person-to-person contact. Any technology that intrudes on either the opportunity for social contact or personal privacy is not likely to be very well accepted nor productive over the long run. A period of adjustment to the new technology that allows and encourages the development of new social channels should be fostered by any company making such changes.

Workstations and microcomputer systems, particularly those that link many users in diverse and geographically distant locations, will affect how users relate and respond to each other. Corporations cannot afford to ignore this vital socialization issue. In a *wired world,* communicating our feelings and our essential humanity will be every bit as important as communicating sterile data.

17.8 THE REAL REVOLUTION

Almost from the inception of the first working model, the computer has been hailed as the single most important invention of the twentieth century, presumably for its ability to expand, amplify, and enhance human intelligence. Yet, in comparison to any present-day computer, those earliest machines were functionally primitive, limited in power, unreliable, and impossibly difficult to work with.

Over the ensuing decades great advances have been made to improve the function, power, and reliability of modern mainframe computers, but their complexity has still largely rendered them inaccessible to all but the most knowledgeable and skillfully trained. Before the microcomputer and certain interactive end-user systems came on the scene, no noncomputing individual could ever hope to use or make use of the enormous power of a computer.

Now all that has changed. The microcomputer has given the gift of computing to all who wish it. Things will never be the same again.

The microcomputer has now long passed the point at which it could be dismissed as a fad. It is fast becoming an integral part of our work, homes, and recreation. Where it will all lead, no one can be sure.

Already described by such terms as "the tool of the century," "pivotal technology," and "the springboard into the information age," the changes to be wrought by microcomputer technology are only starting to make themselves known. In addition to uncounted applications in the business world, the microcomputer is making tremendous inroads into engineering, medicine, education, law, and the arts.

What profound social changes the microcomputer may show us in days to come are yet to be discovered, but there can be no doubt that they will occur. There are intimations that computers in general will affect the coming era to the same magnitude that the printing press, the mails, the telegraph, telephone, and television, the automobile, and jet travel have all affected earlier ones.

The real revolution is not only that we have a new technology that will give to us as individuals the once denied computing capabilities, but that microcomputers will in their future role serve as a new instrument of access to the information of the world and as a new medium of information exchange. They will provide a powerful new kind of access and expression that are fundamental to a free and progressive society.

And there will also come new responsibilities. Microcomputer technology, like every powerful technology before it, can be used for evil as well as for good. Such power given into the hands of mere mortals imposes a moral obligation on each an every one of us, user and nonuser alike. The wise use of this technology, like any other, will require an awareness of its potential for abuse and vigilance against its misuse.

The information era is well upon us. The explosive proliferation of data and information makes little sense unless we as human beings can find some efficient new ways of using it and turning it to our advantage. It is imperative that we seize on every means that can help us deal with the increasing flood of information. It is essential that we employ the technologies that will help us expand our most fundamental human resource, our intelligence and our ability to think.

The future of microcomputers is stretched out before us. Whatever future we wish to create is possible with the right vision. Already we have a great base of resources from which to build that future. The extraordinary accomplishments of the microcomputer industry, the rapid acceptance of personal computing by the general public, and the innovative ways that microcomputers have been put to use both personally and professionally over the past ten years are in and of themselves phenomenal. But the past *is* only prologue. What we have seen and heard to date is no more than the sounding of reveille. The revolution is just beginning.

APPENDIX

A

The Binary Number System

It is not necessary to possess great technical knowledge about microcomputers to use them. But users who do make the effort to understand *how* a computer works, at least conceptually, will learn faster, will find themselves in a better position to solve problems when they arise, and will intuitively understand *why* hardware and software are designed as they are. In short, they will become more effective users.

The binary number system is fundamental to all digital computers (which includes microcomputers). This short narrative describes how the binary number system works and explains how to calculate the decimal equivalent of any binary number.

THE DECIMAL NUMBER SYSTEM: A QUICK REVIEW

We are all familiar with the *decimal number system,* and since the *binary number system* works in a similar fashion, we can begin there. Refreshing our memory about how the decimal number system works can be helpful.

The decimal system has numbers that look like this:

$$5 \quad 14 \quad 36 \quad 104 \quad 2,687 \quad 1,268,309$$

There is nothing special about these particular numbers. They are just given as examples. Each of these numbers consists of combinations of one or more of the digits 0, 1, 2, 3, 4, 5, 6, 7, 8, and 9. Some numbers have only one digit. The largest number given as an example has seven. By increasing the number of digits, a number can be expanded indefinitely.

The third example, 36, has two digits. Its value is thirty-six. The 3 and the 6 represent the value thirty-six because of their respective positions in the number. The position of a digit within a number tells us what value that number should represent. In the *decimal number system*, the values of the *positions* are:

3   6

tens   ones

The value positions are read from *right to left*. Six is in the *ones* position and represents the value 6. Three is in the *tens* position and represents the value 30. And, of course, 30 plus 6 equals the value thirty-six.

The same *place values* can be expanded indefinitely from right to left as shown in this example:

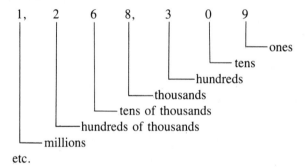

All this discussion so far should sound familiar. You have learned it all before in elementary school arithmetic. But having these concepts fresh in mind makes understanding the binary number system quite easy.

THE BINARY NUMBER SYSTEM

A binary number looks like this:

100101

or this

111

or this

10000000

or this

$$101011$$

Binary numbers only contain the digits 1 and 0 (one and zero). A binary number can have as few as one digit or as many as are necessary. Binary numbers, like decimal numbers, are made larger by adding more digits. For example, the binary number

$$101$$

is larger (represents a higher numerical value) than this binary number:

$$11$$

Binary numbers, like decimal numbers, represent different values because of their relative positions. But in the decimal number system, *positions* moving to the left increase by a factor of 10. That is, each position in a decimal number is ten times greater than the position to the immediate right. (The decimal number system is also called the base ten number system.)

And so it is with binary number system: *positions* moving to the left increase not by ten but *by a factor of 2*. That is, each position in a binary number is two times greater than the position to the immediate right. (The binary number system is also called the base two number system.)

The beginning place values of the binary number system are as follows:

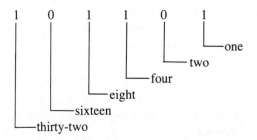

Of course, they continue indefinitely to the left.

In this particular example, the binary number 101101 represents the value 45. This is how it works. A 1 (one) in a given position indicates that the place value for that position *is to be counted*. A 0 (zero) in a given position indicates that the place value for that position is *not* to be counted.

The tally can be made like this:

$$
\begin{array}{cccccc}
1 & 0 & 1 & 1 & 0 & 1 \\
\downarrow & \downarrow & \downarrow & \downarrow & \downarrow & \downarrow \\
(\,32\,+ & 0\,+ & 8\,+ & 4\,+ & 0\,+ & 1 \qquad = 45)
\end{array}
$$

Looking at a simpler example,

10

signifies that a two value is counted, but not a one value; so

1   0

↓   ↓

(2 + 0   = 2)

Or this example,

1101

signifies that an eight value is counted, a four value is counted, a two value is not counted, and a one value is counted; so

1   1   0   1

↓   ↓   ↓   ↓

(8 + 4 + 0 + 1   = 13)

The process of calculating the (decimal) value of a binary number is simply a matter of adding the binary place value for each position in the binary number that contains a 1.

THE PRACTICAL USE OF BINARY NUMBERS

This series of values

1
2
4
8
16
32
64
128
256
512
1024

is referred to repeatedly in microcomputer technical literature. For instance, memory capacities are given as 64K bytes (thousands of characters of storage), 128K bytes, 256K bytes, and so on. The actual number of bytes is greater than these numbers indicate (64K bytes of memory is actually 65,536 bytes), but binary multiples are easier to remember and are used as a kind of shorthand.

APPENDIX

B

Outline of a Year-End Report

A year-end-report should minimally identify (1) objectives (usually those established previously through project or other planning efforts), (2) activities undertaken to achieve the objectives, and (3) the outcomes, results, and achievements resulting from the activities undertaken. Some reports also include "recommendations for future action" as a fourth category.

In general there should be a one-to-one correspondence between objectives, activities, and results. The report may be subdivided into sections treating different types of objectives (e.g., hardware acquisition, software acquisition, software development) or may describe objectives/activities/results for company departments, divisions, or some other organization unit.

A basic end-of-year report outline is outlined next:

Section 1:

Objective: [Statement of first objective]

Activities Undertaken:

[Appropriate narrative describing what was done to accomplish the first objective]

Results/Outcomes:

[Appropriate narrative describing what happened as a result of the activity, benefits to the company, or reasons why the objective could not be accomplished]

Recommendations: (optional)

[Appropriate narrative suggesting what
future actions should be taken to continue or expand benefits to the company,
or to resolve problems encountered]

Section 2:

Objective: [Statement of second objective]

Activities Undertaken:

[Appropriate narrative describing what was done to accomplish the second objective]

Results/Outcomes:

[Appropriate narrative describing what happened as a result of the activity, benefits to the company, or reasons why the objective could not be accomplished]

Recommendations: (optional)

[Appropriate narrative suggesting what future actions should be taken to continue or expand benefits to the company, or to resolve problems encountered]

Section 3:
And so on.

Managers who create such reports should keep well in mind who will be reading the report and why. They should provide the minimal level of factual detail that will help others judge the benefits accruing to the company as a result of the effort and resources expended and/or point out the problems that prevented more positive results. They should place themselves figuratively in the reader's shoes and ask, "If I were reading this report, what would make me feel satisfied that a good job had been done, or what problems occurred that I could help resolve in the future?"

APPENDIX

C

Outline of a Project Impact Study

An impact study is a summary report of innovative project or projectlike activities occurring over a period of several months (such as the recent introduction and use of microcomputer technology) that have had significant effects (an impact) on normal company operations. The impact study differs from a periodic report (like the year-end report described in Appendix B) in that it is only done once, and it does not usually make reference to specific objectives.

The impact study outline presented here consists of five sections, each of which addresses one of the five questions

- What has happened? What microcomputer activities have taken place to date?
- Who is involved? Who is using or is otherwise involved with microcomputers?
- What does it cost? What has been spent and on what?
- What are the results? Any benefits or drawbacks?
- What now? What are the implications for the future?

The suggested contents of a microcomputer project impact study are as follows:

Introduction

A. [Briefly summarize the origins of microcomputer use in the company and the occasion for the report]
B. [Briefly summarize the information to be presented in this report; see the preceding five questions]

Section I: microcomputer activities to date

A. [List major activities that have taken place; give credit for who has done what for what purpose]
B. [List the microcomputer user support services offered]
C. [Provide data or graphs showing the numbers of people using those services; the most impressive data are those that show successive monthly increases]
C. [If appropriate and there are sufficient staff to warrant it, provide an organizational chart describing the support service staff/organization]
D. [Describe any new facilities, how they are being used, and by whom]
E. [List the number and the dollar value of acquired microcomputer hardware systems company wide]
F. [List the number and the dollar value of acquired microcomputer software company wide]

Section II: employee involvement

For each department, or division, as appropriate:

A. [Department name, users' names, users' titles, and current microcomputer applications]
B. [Chart or graph showing increase in numbers of users and/or applications for that department]
C. [List new hardware/software acquired]

Section III: company investment

A. [Provide a summary of expenditures to date:]

Hardware	$ 00000.00
Software	00000.00
Staff Salaries (if relevant)	00000.00
Facilities (if relevant)	00000.00
Training/Technical Support	00000.00
Other Related Expenses	00000.00
Total investment to date:	$ 00000.00

Section IV: return on investment

A. [Provide data supporting tangible benefits to company]
B. [Provide written comments/testimony of users, supervisors, and managers supporting tangible and intangible benefits to themselves/their job/the company]
C. [Provide data comparing departments using microcomputers with those not using microcomputers, if relevant and available]

Section V: implications for the future

A. [Where the benefits outweigh the costs, propose doing more of the same, encouraging more users to use the technology, etc.]
B. [Where the costs outweigh the benefits or the expected results have been disappointing, propose doing something different; address the larger issues and problems that justify the use of microcomputer technology]
C. [Discuss changing conditions or future events that relate to microcomputer technology and its use]

D

Model Policy Document

MICROCOMPUTER USER'S HANDBOOK

Prepared by the
Microcomputer Resource Center
for employees of SuperCorp[1]

---

[1]A fictitious company.

Contents

BACKGROUND

SuperCorp believes that microcomputer technology is an important information and data-processing resource for the company and is committed to its use. Microcomputers provide a great potential for increasing the productivity of a large variety of corporate activities, including financial management, management and decisionmaking, data processing, word processing, and other important company operations.

This booklet is designed to communicate important microcomputer-related information to you and other employees who are currently using microcomputers or who anticipate using them in the near future. It describes the kinds of services that are provided to support you as a microcomputer user, and it outlines the company's policies that govern microcomputer use.

This *Microcomputer User's Handbook* is intended only as an introduction. It cannot provide all the answers that you as a new microcomputer user might have. If you have additional questions that are not answered in this book, contact any staff member of the Microcomputer Resource Center.

CORPORATE MICROCOMPUTER RESOURCES

Purposes

Microcomputers are becoming a way of life at SuperCorp. While they have only been in use since 1982, they have already improved the manner in which many jobs are done. Because they have the potential to increase productivity, to make certain jobs easier, and to improve information processing efficiency in general, many more microcomputers will be put into use over the next few years.

But the company recognizes that microcomputers are "high technology." Their use requires special knowledge and skills. And even though more and more employees will be using microcomputers in the coming months, the company does not expect them to "go it alone." Help and assistance will be provided to all users.

The Microcomputer Resource Center

SuperCorp has organized a special assistance unit called the Microcomputer Resource Center (MRC). The purpose of the MRC is to coordinate and assist in the appropriate use of microcomputer technology within the company.

The MRC is staffed with experienced individuals who are knowledgeable about all aspects of corporate microcomputing applications and are familiar with all the systems used throughout the company.

The MRC is centrally located in [company location]. Staff members are available during regular working hours to answer questions and to assist you with microcomputer-related applications.

MRC SERVICES

The MRC offers a variety of services including:

- Assistance in the preparation of requests to acquire and use a microcomputer
- Assistance in the selection and purchase of microcomputer software programs
- Assistance in the selection and purchase of microcomputer hardware equipment
- Assistance in setting up, operating, and maintaining microcomputer systems
- Training on microcomputer operation and related topics
- General assistance on microcomputer-related problems

Microcomputer Software Services

The MRC provides microcomputer users with several software-related services. Software services include:

- Demonstrations of new software
- Recommendations of specific software
- Assistance in using a particular software program
- Assistance in determining and assuring software (file) compatibility when more than one program uses the same file
- Evaluations of new software releases
- Operation of a company library of software programs and documentation

Microcomputer Hardware Services

The MRC provides microcomputer users with assistance in the selection and use of hardware. Hardware services include:

- Suggestions on the best kinds of hardware to do various jobs
- Demonstrations of different microcomputers, printers, plotters, and other peripheral equipment
- Unpacking, setup, and checkout of new equipment
- Repair and maintenance of equipment
- Troubleshooting of technical problems

System Acquisition

Company policy requires that all new microcomputer applications and requests for the acquisition of microcomputer systems be planned and reviewed in advance. A special Microcomputer Acquisitions Review board has been established to review all microcomputer-related requests. The purpose of this board is not to stifle the use of microcomputers, but to ensure that the company invests in appropriate systems that will do the job and are compatible with other computer and communications systems in the company.

A formal procedure for planning and review of microcomputer-related acquisitions has been approved by management and is administered through the MRC. Any employee considering the use of a microcomputer for a job where microcomputers have not previously been used is required to follow this procedure.

This procedure is designed to collect specific information that will help you identify clearly what system components will best do the job, and information that will aid the Microcomputer Acquisitions Review Board judge the appropriateness of the application and the appropriateness of the requested hardware and software.

MRC staff members will work closely with you to complete the procedure. Your full cooperation with staff members will greatly expedite the acquisition of an appropriate system.

The following is a chronological checklist of steps in the procedure that require your participation:

1. Visit the MRC and discuss your intended use of a microcomputer with a member of the staff. Try out some of the demonstration systems, if you like. Ask lots of questions. Be sure and ask for a copy of the form called the Microcomputer Requirements Analysis and System Definition. (The form is easier to complete than it is to say. You may even have fun filling it out.)

2. Spend some time thinking about how you would use a microcomputer on a day-to-day basis. Think about what you *do* want it to do and what you *don't* want it to do. Complete the Microcomputer Requirements Anal-

ysis and System Definition form and return it to the MRC. Set up a time to go over the form with a staff member.

3. Review your answers on the form with a staff member. If hardware and/or software are available for preview, spend an hour or two getting familiar. Try out various programs. Talk to other employees who are using similar hardware and software.

4. Once you are satisfied that you have identified the appropriate system for your particular application, complete the Purchase Request form and attach the other form and any further information you think would be useful to the board. Submit the memo and forms to a member of the MRC staff to begin the formal review of your request. (Your request will be reviewed for completeness and forwarded on to the Microcomputer Acquisitions Review Board.)

Once your request has been reviewed and has all authorizing signatures, you will be notified by a MRC staff member who will then prepare the appropriate purchase order. You will be notified when the system components are received. A staff member will arrange a time with you to set up any equipment and make the new system operational, to provide any training or initial assistance you may request, and to wish you "happy microcomputing"!

User Training and Assistance

The most important function of the MRC is to provide training and assistance to microcomputer users. Users of new microcomputer systems are expected by the company to participate in training classes or to otherwise demonstrate their operational competence.

The following training programs are offered periodically:

- Demonstrations of microcomputer hardware and software
- Classroom workshops on computer applications and programming
- Classroom workshops and seminars on advanced techniques
- Individual and small-group instruction on specific microcomputer systems (by special arrangement)

A schedule of training programs is always posted on the MRC bulletin-board and is announced through the company newsletter, *SuperCorp Communicator*.

SPECIAL RESTRICTIONS

Nonauthorized Use

Nonauthorized use is defined as the use of microcomputers for purposes not officially sanctioned by the company. Nonauthorized uses include (but are not necessarily limited to) playing games on company time, writing programs for personal use or noncompany related applications. Any questions you have about the legitimacy of any particular use of the microcomputer should be referred to the next level of management above your own level.

Microcomputer Location and Off-site Use

It is generally assumed that microcomputers will be physically located in the user's department or at a designated work location. Once set up in a specified location, microcomputer equipment should not be moved without first consulting with a MRC staff member. This especially applies to microcomputers linked to a network and those with hard-disk storage units. (Moving disk units without precautionary steps can permanently damage disk units and result in a loss of stored data.)

Under certain circumstances, company microcomputers may be used off site. Such use requires the written approval of the department head. Use of company-owned equipment off site may increase the user's liability for damage, loss, or theft. Contact the MRC for Off-site Microcomputer Use forms and for additional information relating to off-site use.

Copyright Infringement

All software programs purchased by the company are protected by copyright laws. These laws make it illegal to copy programs for any use other than for a single system. Some software licenses allow special backup copies to be made to guard against damage to the disk and loss of the program, but these backup copies are not to be given to or used by other microcomputer users.

Any copy not specifically permitted by the copyright owner's licensing agreement (on file in the MRC) constitutes copyright infringement, an illegal act that is punishable by imprisonment of one year and/or fines up to $10,000 plus statutory damages.

SuperCorp policy specifically forbids the willful making, distribution, or acceptance of any unauthorized copies by employees acting on behalf of the company. Violation of this policy can result in termination of employment.

The issues surrounding fair use and copyright infringement are complex. If you have any concerns or questions about the legitimacy of making software copies, do not make copies until you have consulted with the director of the MRC. The director may refer your questions to the copyright holder directly or consult with corporate legal counsel.

User-developed Software

It is company policy and a condition of employment that any discoveries or inventions made by employees using company resources (including salaried time) are the sole property of SuperCorp. This policy applies to employee-created software programs. Any microcomputer programs created using company resources are automatically company property.

All software, documentation, and copies of the same must be left with the department head upon termination or transfer to another department.

Access to the Corporate Database

The use of microcomputers to access the SuperCorp central computer systems and databases requires the prior approval of the director of Management Information Systems. Microcomputers require special circuitry, cabling, or data communications equipment to access another computer and must be specially equipped to allow access.

Also, microcomputer users who have a justified need to access corporate databases will be issued a log-on code and private password to permit access to authorized files and systems. All microcomputer-to-mainframe computer communications should be discussed with a member of the MRC staff.

MAKING MICROCOMPUTERS WORK FOR OUR COMPANY

While the company finds it necessary to invoke a few policies that govern microcomputer use, it is believed that these policies will make microcomputer use easier for everyone and protect the interests of the company at the same time.

Microcomputing is relatively new, and the company expects to learn much about how best to use this technology as time goes on; but the most important resource in microcomputing is *you*. You must help us discover the best uses of this new tool. As you work with hardware and software systems day in and day out, think about how other jobs might be done better, more effectively, more efficiently, and for a greater cost savings to the company. Give us your ideas and suggestions. We need *your* help, too.

E

Microcomputer Requirements Analysis and System Definition
(A Model Form)

**MICROCOMPUTER REQUIREMENTS ANALYSIS
AND SYSTEMS DEFINITION**

SECTION I: IDENTIFYING INFORMATION

Name: Phone:
Title or Job Designation:
Department:
Supervisor's Name: Phone:

SECTION II: REQUIREMENTS ANALYSIS

Please answer all questions as completely as possible. Use additional sheets as necessary.

1. Are you currently having a work problem that you think a microcomputer could help solve? If so, describe this problem in some detail.

2. State briefly what you want a microcomputer to do for you.

3. Describe how you are doing that job/task/procedure at the present time:

4. How would the use of a microcomputer affect that job/task/procedure?

5. How much data would you be working with *at one time*? Estimate an approximate number of pages:

6. Where do the data come from that you plan to use? Yourself? Other employees? The corporate database (i.e., the main computer system)? In what form are these data provided to you?

7. What would you produce with a microcomputer? What kinds of documents, reports, etc. would you generate?

8. Who gets the output in addition to yourself?

9. What kinds of processes would be required of the microcomputer? Would you be doing calculations? Editing or reformatting text documents? Creating graphics? Communicating with other microcomputer users or the main computer system? Do you need to store and retrieve records or files of data?

10. How often would you be using a microcomputer? Every day? Approximately how many times a month or hours per week:

11. How much time typically elapses between the time you receive data to be processed until the time you are expected to produce a report, etc.? How urgent are the jobs for which you would use a microcomputer? Are these jobs particularly time critical?

12. Where will the microcomputer be located? Will anyone else be using this system besides yourself? If so, who?

13. How accurate must the output be? Is there any room for error? Is accuracy a critical issue for you?

14. Will the use of a microcomputer affect your co-workers or affect the way in which they do their jobs? If so, discuss in detail:

15. List the specific benefits that you believe will accrue to yourself, your co-workers, and the company in general:

16. Have you used and worked with microcomputers or other computers before? How would you describe your level of knowledge about microcomputers and your operating skill? Rank beginner? Modest experience? Considerable experience? Expert user?

SECTION III: SYSTEM DEFINITION

List and describe the components and estimated cost of the microcomputer system you are requesting:

Item   **Estimated Cost**

Hardware:

Total Estimated Hardware Cost: $

Software:

Total Estimated Software Cost: $

Supplies and
Miscellaneous:

Total Estimated Supplies/Misc. Cost: $

===

Total Estimated System Cost:

F

Preliminary Considerations for the Selection of Microcomputer Software

The selection of microcomputer software for use by corporate users requires that a number of factors be considered, especially where the operating systems are different and where the skill levels of users are dissimilar. Critical areas that need to be considered are compatibility with the operating system, hardware requirements made by the software, error handling, data compatibility, software copyright and licensing restrictions, the type of user for which the software was designed, user and technical documentation, friendliness of the design and user interfaces, uses of hardware features like color and graphics, and the kind of after-the-sale support that may be expected from the vendor or software house that created the software.

The following questions are designed to focus specific attention on these crucial issues during the software selection process:

SYSTEM REQUIREMENTS AND DOS COMPATIBILITY

- What DOS (disk operating system) will the software work with?
- How much memory is required?
- How much memory is needed as a practical necessity?

- Does the software require color and graphics capabilities?
- Does the software require specific hardware capabilities (such as plotters, graphics boards, joysticks or special input devices)?
- Does the software require that a diskette remain in the disk drive during operation? Does the software require two drives?
- Is the software resident in memory at all times? If memory resident, is the software under consideration compatible with other memory resident programs?

ERROR HANDLING

- Does the software permit the user to recover from errors without losing files or data entered to that point?
- Does the program feature an "un-do" command that will allow the user to reverse the previous command or restore the program to an earlier state?

DATA COMPATIBILITY

- Does the software generate data files that are compatible with those used in other programs? [Some programs produce data in the DIF (Data Interchange Format) while others produce data in the ASCII (American Standard Code for Information Interchange), and there are still other data formats. In different formats, it is not possible to transfer data from one program to another. For example, data from a spreadsheet using the DIF format could not be transferred into a word processing program to be included in a report because almost all word-processing programs use the ASCII format.]

COPY PROTECTION AND LICENSING RESTRICTIONS

- Is this program copy protected?
- Will it be possible to make working copies so that the original may be kept as a master? [There is a trend by some software houses to not copy protect their software. It is done for the convenience of the user even though it makes illegal copying (piracy) easy. Since it is in the best interest of users to make backup copies, software purchasers should encourage this practice by buying noncopy protected software, all other considerations being equal. However, it is incumbent upon companies to enforce policies that require employees to be scrupulously honest in the copying of copyrighted software and to use it only as permitted by the licensing agreement.]

• Can this software program be installed on a hard-disk system?

• Can it be used in a microcomputer network? If so, what additional licensing fees are required? [Many software programs are designed to be used exclusively with floppy disk systems and cannot be used on hard-disk systems. Also, some software licenses specifically forbid software to be used in a network where multiple users would have access to the software.]

USER LEVEL

• For what level user is the software designed? Experienced users? Those with a strong computer background? Novices? What assumptions does the software seem to make about users?

• Who is the software intended for in the company? How experienced are these users?

DOCUMENTATION AND USER-FRIENDLY DESIGN

• Does the software have complete, easy-to-understand documentation? Better still, does it feature on-screen help messages and are these messages really useful?

• Is the user information separate from technical information?

• Does the software have user-friendly features like menus and full-English prompts or easy to remember and execute commands? If expected users are experienced, will they want menu-oriented programs or would they prefer command-oriented programs?

• Does the program intuitively make sense to the user or does every command seem awkward? Are commands easy to recall without having to look them up in a manual or user's guide?

FULL-FEATURED/ENHANCEMENTS

• Does the software take advantage of the full capabilities of the computer system, such as the use of function keys, screen enhancements, color, and other features where appropriate?

• Does the software (or hardware) permit printing the contents of the screen on the printer?

VENDOR SUPPORT

- What is the vendor's or developer's policy regarding after-sale support? Can users get technical assistance and questions answered from the software developer directly?

Index